# Kent
## MURDERS

LINDA STRATMANN

*To Liz, my Canadian soul mate*

First published 2009

The History Press
The Mill, Brimscombe Port
Stroud, Gloucestershire, GL5 2QG
www.thehistorypress.co.uk

Reprinted 2009, 2010, 2011

© Linda Stratmann, 2009

The right of Linda Stratmann to be identified as the Author of this work has been asserted in accordance with the Copyrights, Designs and Patents Act 1988.

All rights reserved. No part of this book may be reprinted or reproduced or utilised in any form or by any electronic, mechanical or other means, now known or hereafter invented, including photocopying and recording, or in any information storage or retrieval system, without the permission in writing from the Publishers.

British Library Cataloguing in Publication Data.
A catalogue record for this book is available from the British Library.

ISBN 978 0 7509 4811 1

Typesetting and origination by The History Press
Printed in Great Britain

# CONTENTS

|   | Acknowledgements | 4 |
|---|---|---|
| 1. | Brotherly Love<br>*Sheldwich, 1655* | 5 |
| 2. | Dead of Night<br>*Chislehurst, 1813* | 21 |
| 3. | The Saviour of the People<br>*Canterbury, 1838* | 35 |
| 4. | The Body on the Beach<br>*Ramsgate, 1859* | 52 |
| 5. | The Man Who Wanted to be Hanged<br>*Chatham, 1862* | 66 |
| 6. | The Unwanted Wife<br>*Cudham & Penge, 1877* | 81 |
| 7. | The Veiled Lady<br>*Yalding, 1881* | 97 |
| 8. | The Mysterious Death of Dr Lyddon<br>*Faversham, 1890* | 113 |
| 9. | A Tragedy of Reckless Folly<br>*Whitstable, 1926* | 128 |
| 10. | Shore Leave<br>*Gravesend, 1926* | 143 |
|   | *Bibliography & References* | 155 |
|   | *Index* | 158 |

# ACKNOWLEDGEMENTS

I would like to extend my grateful thanks to the staff of the British Library, Colindale Newspaper Library and the National Archives who have as always been unfailingly helpful. My thanks must also go to the churchwardens of St Nicholas, Chislehurst, and St Michael and All Angels, Throwley, for taking the time to show me the lovely interiors and monuments of those beautiful churches; to John Endicott, curator of the Kent Police Museum, for supplying some wonderful photographs and allowing me to photograph John Mears' staff; and to Mrs Shahida Afzal of Penenden Heath Lodge for her hospitality.

I would like to say thank you also to all the members of the Forest Writers' group who have listened to my readings and made many helpful comments on my work. Lastly, but by no means least, I must thank my husband Gary, whose assistance as driver, photographer, companion, and maker of wonderful coffee, I could not have done without.

# 1

# BROTHERLY LOVE

## *Sheldwich, 1655*

When Sir Ralph Freeman, Lord Mayor of London, died in 1634 he left a will which made a carefully planned disposal of his lands. Only one of his children, his daughter Jane, had survived infancy, and in 1620, aged eighteen, she had married twenty-one-year-old George Sondes. Sir Ralph approved of the match. George was a steady serious young man, with good family connections and land of his own. In 1626 he was knighted at the coronation of King Charles I. Sir Ralph must have hoped that Jane and George would have a large family, but many of their children died in infancy. By the time of Sir Ralph's death the couple had only two living children, both sons; Freeman Sondes, named after his grandfather, was born in 1629, and George in 1633. Sir Ralph's will ensured that his son-in-law would inherit substantial properties, but he also made provision for his two grandsons, who would not have to wait for the death of their vigorous young father to set up households of their own. To Freeman, his favourite, he left several parcels of land, and to baby George a rather smaller inheritance, an interest in some property in Devon. It was provided that if Freeman should predecease George junior then Freeman's share would go to his younger brother.

Six months after Sir Ralph's death, four-year-old Freeman died; all his inheritance rights passing to his brother. In 1636 Jane Sondes bore another son. He, too, was called Freeman. It was customary in Kent for estates to be divided equally between male heirs, but more than a hundred years earlier, the Sondes family, in common with many others, had sought a special Act of Parliament to avoid splitting its lands. Under the provisions of Sir Ralph's will, therefore, the second Freeman Sondes had no inheritance.

The Sondes family owned 6,500 acres of land, on which stood many properties including two fine manor houses in Kent; Town Place at Throwley, where the head of the family usually resided; and Lees Court near Sheldwich, occupied by the heir.

Although Sir George inherited Town Place on the death of his father in 1632, and lived there for a time, he always regarded Lees Court as his true home.

Sir George was devoted to three things in his life: religion, the management of his estate, and his family. He later claimed that during the years of his marriage he had remained faithful to his wife. 'I never had illegitimate issue, not ever had carnal knowledge of any woman, save of my own wife; not of her, but as was fitting for procreation ...' Sir George was a dutiful, rather than affectionate husband, always doing what he thought was for the best and never swerving from his strict religious principles. He believed in fairness, justice and order. When Jane died in 1637 Sir George continued to exercise this extraordinary restraint, choosing not to remarry. A second family would not only cost money, which he felt would be better employed enhancing his estates, but might well lead to problems of inheritance.

Besides the care of his estates, Sir George had political and administrative duties both national and local, with which to busy himself. He entered parliament in 1628, and there were terms as sheriff and deputy lieutenant of the county. It was during the 1630s that he commenced a programme of reconstruction at Lees Court, rebuilding in a style reminiscent of that of Inigo Jones. With the outbreak of Civil War in 1642, Sir George, nominally a Royalist, did his best not to become involved. So carefully did he sit on the fence, that for a time neither side claimed him as its own, then in 1643 he was arrested, for no offence of which he was aware, and had his estate sequestrated by Parliament, the income used to finance the war. Sir George was confined to the Tower of London, where he was to remain until his release in 1650. He later estimated that the fines and depredations had cost him £40,000, yet he was still able to continue the building works at Lees Court, which were completed in 1652.

*Lees Court, c. 1905. (Author's collection)*

With his two sons approaching manhood, Sir George might have considered how best to adjust the inequality of their fortunes. Splitting the estate was not an option he could condone, but even after the damage done by years of sequestration, it was not impossible for him to find some funds to set aside for Freeman. For reasons which he never adequately explained, however, he chose not to do so. Sir George never swerved from the opinion that when his sons were young, he had spoiled them; '... they were tender and weak, and when I had buried many other and had only them two, I confess I was more fond and indulgent, and gave more way to them than otherwise I should have done.' During his years in the Tower, however, he had rarely seen his sons, and when he was released they were both studying at Sydney Sussex College, Cambridge. It was not until 1651 that he was able to make up for lost time, and he plunged eagerly into doing all the things that had been denied to him by his imprisonment. He and the boys spent some months in London, where he devoted himself to completing their education, bringing masters to teach them singing, dancing, fencing, mathematics and riding. On Sundays he took them to hear sermons, and made sure to discuss what was said afterwards to ensure that the lesson had been understood.

The temptations offered by London were varied and enormous, and Sir George saw it as his duty to ensure that his boys did not keep bad company or indulge in 'not fitting sports'. He believed that his own example had dissuaded them both from debauchery, 'For, I thank heaven, no man can tax me for swearing, drinking, whoring or gaming.' He was not entirely successful, and saw to his sorrow that both his sons had become devotees of cockfighting and spent far too much on clothes, but was comforted by the fact that George rarely drank and Freeman could not abide it.

It had been Sir George's intentions to send his eldest son to France to complete his education, but France was then going through a period of unrest and, in view of the potential dangers to a traveller, he decided against it. By the end of 1652 the family was able to settle in Lees Court, at a moderately safe distance from the diversions of London.

Thus far in their history there appear to have been no serious differences between the two boys, and their father had made no distinction between them. Despite the age gap, they were largely schooled together and were at Cambridge together, Freeman entering when he was just fourteen.

It is often the case that siblings are unalike both in appearance and character, where one more closely resembles the mother and one the father. This may have been the case with the Sondes brothers. Perhaps the elder boy reminded Sir George of his late wife, while Freeman, too much like his father, was a mirror of his own youthful faults and follies which he had learned to govern. Contemporary accounts suggest that George was both better looking and better liked than his brother. Writer Richard Faber was convinced that a seventeenth-century portrait of two young men originating from Lees Court is of the brothers, and if that is the case, one is handsome and elegant, the other smaller, with fleshier, less attractive features.

George certainly knew how to charm young women. In 1654 Sir George discovered that his elder son, now at his majority, and able to take possession of his inheritance, had been conducting a romance (whether it was actually an affair will never be known) with his first cousin, Anne Delaune, who lived an hour's ride away. Determined that his son could do far better, Sir George immediately put a stop to the relationship. George must have known that the law of primogeniture, and Sir George's unwillingness to split the estate, made him his father's principal heir. Sir George may well have taken the opportunity to state that in the event of a marriage which he could not approve, all that could change. Young George saw where his interests lay and obeyed his father without a quibble, breaking off the relationship. It was as if his affection for Anne had never existed. There were rumours that George and Anne had actually married, but Sir George did not believe that they were, and the most that the lady could claim was that marriage had been promised. Sir George was plainly relieved that young George was 'ready to hearken to his father's advice'. Certainly his elder son seemed outwardly virtuous, and paid close attention to his religious devotions. 'I am confident all the world could not make him commit a known sin,' wrote his father, describing George as 'affable mild and soft' in nature, and well loved by both friends and acquaintances. Certainly George was out to enjoy life, but only as long as he could do so without rocking the boat. The opinion of others, especially his father, was of vital importance to him. Whether his devotions were genuinely felt or were a part of his campaign to stay in his father's good books, will never be known. By 1655 he was consoling himself with a mistress in London.

Although Sir George had made every effort to bring up his sons in the same way, a pivotal change occurred when Freeman left college, for his father made it very clear that he intended to leave his whole estate to his elder son and that Freeman was expected to shift for himself. From that time Sir George exercised a constant pressure upon Freeman to find a profession, to 'study law, or be a merchant, or anything, so he would be something.' Freeman, not perhaps realising that being master of the Sondes estates would not be a life of idle luxury for George, began to realise how vastly different their adult lives were to be, and all from the accident of birth. The feeling of being always second best, the pure unfairness of it all, rankled deeply and ate away at everything that had made Freeman love his brother. He still loved him, but that feeling was now cloaked with a bitter resentment. His sullen bad temper made him increasingly poor company, and Sir George seemed unable to fathom the reason for it, commenting only that Freeman was 'pleasing and courteous to none, but cross-grained to all, as much to his father as any, and I knew not how to break him of it ...' With little to occupy himself, Freeman continued to attend cockfights until they were banned in 1654, and also played cards, and spent enormous sums on clothes. He was no noisy rakehell, nor wildly dissolute – a clergyman later described him as 'very gentle and humble, like a child.' Shy, sullen and unhappy, he found it difficult to win the approval of young women although there was a lady with whom he sometimes played cards, a lady with a fortune of

£300–400 a year. It was rumoured, though never proven, that this lady was his brother's former love, Anne Delaune. Sir George, in contrast with the fury with which he had greeted his elder son's romance, was happy to see this match made and offered to provide an equal income, but Freeman denied that there was any serious intent in the relationship.

Freeman seemed content to mark time until he reached his majority, for he had a small expectation. He believed – and the source of this information is unknown – that he was due to inherit an estate which would provide an income of £1,000 a year (equivalent to £140,000 in today's money). With that sum, Freeman, while remaining resentful of his brother's glittering fortunes, would be content. There was still some friction between Freeman and his father, who was unhappy at his younger son's coming and going at all hours and incessant gambling, but there was no real explosion of rage until the affair of the doublet.

Gorge and Freeman had grey doublets which they wore when out riding. The two garments looked very similar, and when George went away in the spring of 1655 his manservant packed Freeman's doublet by mistake. George wore the doublet, and despite the fact that it was a little too small for him, did not notice the error until later. When he returned to Lees Court after Easter the two young men were talking in George's bedroom when George recalled he still had Freeman's doublet and suggested they exchange. Freeman was in an uncooperative and surly mood, and refused to make the swap. Their father, who was in the next room, overheard the argument and came to see what all the noise was about. On learning the reason for the quarrel, Sir George curtly told his sons to settle the matter. On the following day Freeman was still in truculent mood, unwilling to give way to his favoured older brother. Sir George, rapidly running out of patience, ordered Freeman to hand over his brother's doublet. Freeman refused. 'Nay, now I see it is nothing but wilfulness, only to cross your brother,' said Sir George, exasperated. Freeman's obstinacy had stung Sir George, who seemed incapable of recognising the grievances that lay beneath what appeared to be an argument over a trivial matter. Rather than try and deal with the underlying problems, he decided that a stern lecture was needed to bring his difficult younger son into line. The effect of his words, though he was never able to understand this, made the antagonism Freeman felt for his blameless brother explosively worse:

> These cross and dogged humours of yours, if you continue in them, will ruin you: you need not be so dogged to your brother, for I tell you, if I die you must be beholding to him, and whatever your flatterers tell you of an estate of a thousand pounds a year, or more, that you have, which your father cannot keep from you, I who know better than they, tell you that you have not a groat but what you must be beholding to your father for, and that it is in his power to leave you as little as your uncle Nicholas had left him ...

This was a very telling threat. Nicholas, a half brother of Sir George, had made an unfortunate marriage, had no fortune of his own, and was tolerated as a 'poor relation'.

If Freeman had felt some superiority over Nicholas and his dull existence, he would have been severely shaken by his father's words.

This sudden disappearance of his expectations stunned Freeman, and the more he thought about it the worse it seemed. Not only was there no annuity as he had thought, but he managed to convince himself that his father intended to keep him poor during his lifetime, and, on his death, make him a servant to his brother. If Freeman had gambling debts, which was not unlikely, he now faced the prospect that he would never be able to clear them.

Freeman's unhappiness simmered unpleasantly for a time, and if anything he became rebelliously less amenable to his father's wishes. When further pressed to decide upon a career, he refused to make a decision. A few days afterwards, an open quarrel blew up between Freeman and his father, during which Sir George struck him. The blow was, Sir George later claimed, no more than 'a little pat on the head' and it may have been more humiliating than painful. Freeman's response was to sit down quietly in a chair, without moving or speaking for four or five hours. Emotions must have been boiling in his mind, and it may have been then that he determined not to be a victim of fate and his father's control, but take matters into his own hands. Consumed with misery and resentment, he saw no hope of any kind of happy life either then or in the future; being always too poor to make a good marriage, and forever beholden to his relatives, to whom he would be an object of pity. There was only one situation that could help him achieve what he desired – his brother and father must both die, and it must appear to be the work of intruders.

Freeman was calm enough not to do anything at once. He spent several weeks making his plans, during which time George was frequently away from home, and at the end of May, Sir George was once again arrested as a Royalist and placed in Upnor Castle, where he remained until the end of July.

Freeman's mood had not altered, and he determined on a day of action. On 7 August the assizes would begin at Maidstone. This event would bring many people to the town, increasing the possibility of new criminals in the area, and the constables would have their hands too full dealing with prisoners to worry about possible burglars. All three Sondes would be at Lees Court. The early morning would also be light enough for Freeman to see what he was doing without the aid of a candle, whose light might awaken his sleeping victims. Nothing that happened in the days between his father's return and the assizes changed Freeman's resolve. On Sunday 5 August he crept into the empty kitchen, took a meat cleaver, and hid it in his room. Monday passed without any family friction, Freeman perhaps taking especial care to put on a show of amity, to defuse any suspicion against him. The family said prayers together as usual and went to bed.

Sir George and his elder son slept soundly, but Freeman forced himself to remain awake. It was not yet five in the morning when Freeman took the cleaver and a dagger and crept into his brother's room. George lay on his left side, and Freeman at once struck him on the right side of the head with the heavy blunt back of the cleaver, breaking the skull. It was a mortal blow, but George still lived, and half-

*Upnor castle. (Author's collection)*

awake, dazed and confused, writhed in pain. Freeman later claimed that once he had struck the first blow he would have given all the world to recall it, yet having gone so far he could only continue, and put his stricken brother out of his agony. Again and again he brought the weapon down, five times in all. Each time, there was the sickening sound of bone being crushed, and blood flew all about, flying off the cleaver as he raised it for the last few blows. That should have been enough, but to his horror Freeman saw that his brother, despite being terribly injured, was still alive. As he watched, George rolled onto his back, moaning in pain and distress.

Freeman had begun his murderous mission with the intensity of chilled determination, but he was now revolted by what he had done. All his hatred and resentment of his brother had evaporated, and he realised that he had killed the person he had loved most all his life. As for himself, 'he thought he was for this world utterly undone.' From that moment on, Freeman Sondes was a walking dead man.

There was only one thing he could do for his suffering brother. He took out his dagger and stabbed George seven times in the chest. Still George would not die, still he moaned. Freeman, unable to will himself on to do more, had abandoned all thought of harming his father. He was ready to confess. He threw the cleaver out of the window, put the dagger in his pocket and went to his father's bedroom next door.

Sir George had slept through the noise. With bloodied hands, Freeman shook his father awake. Their words would haunt Sir George for the rest of his life.

'Father, I have killed my brother.'

'What sayest thou? Hast thou, wretch, killed thy brother? Then thou hadst best kill me, too!'

'No, Sir, I have done enough.'

'Why then, you must look to be hanged.'

Sir George leaped out of bed and went at once to his elder son's room, where George, still barely alive, lay moaning in a bed saturated with blood. It was obvious that nothing could be done for him. Freeman appeared to be without emotion, and his father interpreted that as a cold lack of any regret for his actions, but his blank expression was more probably that of a man already contemplating death.

Despite the shock, Sir George took charge of the situation. Calling up his servants he ordered that a Justice be sent for at once, and had a compliant Freeman locked in his bedroom. Soon afterwards, George breathed his last.

It might have been possible for Sir George as a prominent landowner to make some request for lenient treatment for his only son, but he made no attempt to do so. Determinedly, implacably, he took all the steps required to bring Freeman to justice, and made it clear from the outset that he never wanted to set eyes on him again. He insisted that Freeman should not remain another night under the same roof, and before the end of the day the prisoner was removed to a nearby house. The following day he was taken to Maidstone Gaol.

Sir George did, however, pray for his son. The Sondes family prayers pleaded for the Lord to '... soften his hard and stubborn heart, and give him a true sight of his most heinous and bloody sin, and an hearty sorrow for the same.' As a part of the prayer Sir George claimed that he had pardoned Freeman who had 'foully killed his dear son, and ruined him in all his hopes', yet this was the voice of a devout and dutiful Christian addressing his God and his Saviour. As a father, such forgiveness was impossible.

Four days after his death, George Sondes was buried at the church of St Michael and All Angels, Throwley. The circumstances of his death were so shameful to his family that no monument was erected to his memory.

Freeman, in the common prison, 'stenched with the noisome scent of prisoners', was meek and quiet, never complained about his treatment, and gave Mr Foster, the gaoler, no trouble. Freeman was not without friends, and one, Edmund Crisp, the son of local gentry, visited him in gaol, and did all he could for him. It may well have been Edmund's doing that after a day in the stink of the common gaol, Freeman was transferred to Mr Foster's house as was more in keeping with his social status.

On Thursday 7 August Freeman was brought before the justices at Maidstone Assizes, where he was questioned by Sir Thomas Stiles and Sir Michael Livesey. Livesey, as first cousin to Sir George, had a considerable personal interest in the case, but he was also of a vastly different political colour, being one of the signatories to the death warrant of Charles I, and as such would have relished any information to his cousin's detriment. Freeman must have been aware of this, and when asked why he had committed the crime, took the opportunity to place

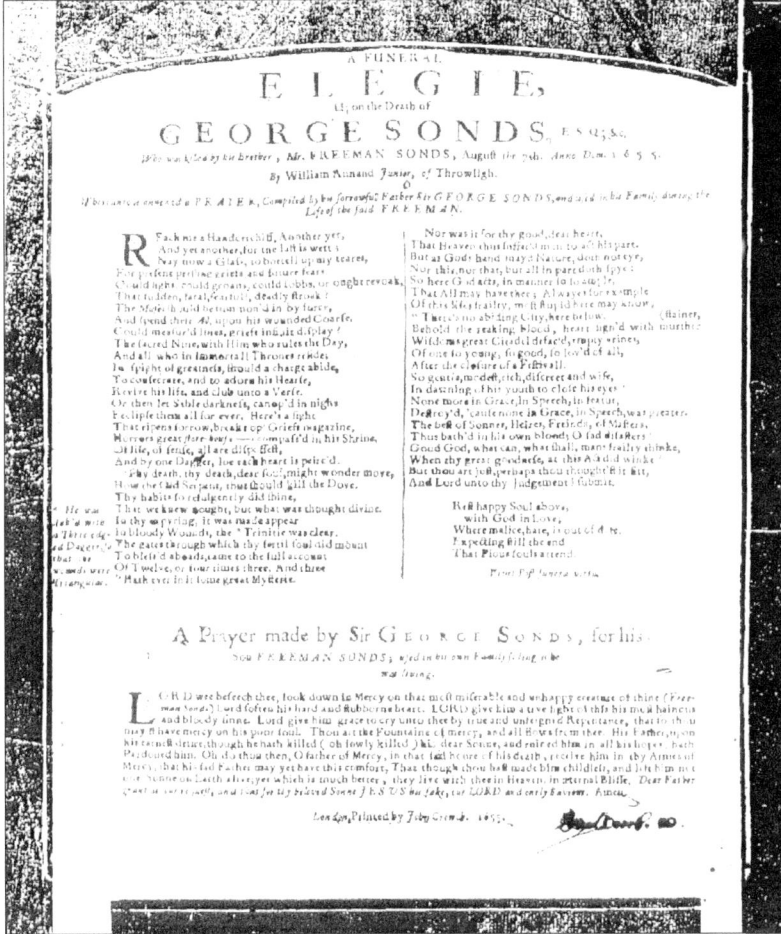

*A Funeral Elegie Upon the Death of George Sonds, Esq. (Author's collection)*

all the blame on his father. Unable to find the courage to kill his father, he had determined to act with all the gentle subservience of a victim and do as much damage to Sir George's reputation as possible. Freeman claimed that his father had kept him short of money (something Sir George vehemently denied) and that following the argument about the doublet he had been threatened with ruin, poverty and a life of servitude to his brother. Sir George freely admitted the hard words he had spoken to Freeman, but insisted that they had been 'spoken to thee for thy amendment, but not for thy hurt!'

Sir George was never able to understand that, despite his obvious affection for both his sons, his unequal treatment of them had had some role to play in the tragedy. 'It is strange to see,' he wrote later, 'how [Freeman] seems to make my hard using of him to be the motive and provocation; whereas it is well known to all, that never a son was treated more tenderly by a father.'

*Church of St Michael and All Angels, Throwley. (Author's collection)*

Freeman calmly pleaded guilty to the murder of his brother and declared himself willing to meet his fate without complaint. He was taken to the condemned cell, where he spent a number of hours in filthy conditions. When asked by a visitor how he could tolerate the stench, he replied mildly that he preferred it to his father's dining room. The visits he received from clergymen while in prison did, however, convince him that his afterlife would be a lot more comfortable if he used his remaining days to make his peace with his father.

The outcome of the trial, which took place before Judge Crook on 10 August, was never in doubt, and Freeman declined to make any further statement about his reasons for committing the crime, or express his remorse, but asked for a petition to be read out. While accepting that it was his fate to be executed, he asked humbly to be allowed a few more days of life, to 'make his peace with God, and reconcile himself to his deservedly and highly offended father.' The judge willingly allowed him until 15 August.

Freeman must have found his last few days on earth some of the pleasantest of his life. Everyone was deeply concerned for him, he had numerous visitors who all took a great interest in his soul, he was transferred back to the comfort of Mr Foster's, he was no longer being harangued by his father to take up some miserable profession, and did not have to endure the mocking presence of the golden boy, the much loved and much hated elder brother. A strange kind of peace descended upon him. Sir George would hardly have recognised his formerly awkward, sullen and argumentative son.

On 13 August, Edmund Crisp helped Freeman compose a formal confession to his crime. In this document he no longer blamed his father, but attributed his sin to that most traditional of impulses; the 'instigation of the devil.' In this confession Freeman deeply regretted his sin against the laws of the land, against society and against God. Nowhere did he mention his father. Nevertheless more than a week after his crime, a time during which he had had no communication with Sir George, he composed a personal letter to his 'most dear and loving father.'

Acknowledging that 'through the heinousness of my offence, I am unworthy to see your face once more in this world,' he begged for 'your pardon, your blessing, and your prayers, which I doubt not to obtain.' His words reveal a trusting confidence in salvation through forgiveness. 'I hope in a very short time to rest in Abraham's bosom, whither my brother is gone before me ... And you, my dear father, shall in God's good time follow after.'

Sir George sent a long and formal reply, addressing the penitent baldly as 'Son Freeman' and stating that he hoped that Freeman was as truly sorry for his crime as his letter stated, and on that basis, 'I do really and fully forgive you ... But ...', and this was a very telling 'but', he added that Freeman would only be received into God's mercy on a true repentance and acknowledgement of his sins,

> ... and that (let me be plain with you) I yet see not in you. For this most detestable fact, you confess indeed that you did it, but, as much as in you lies, lay the provocation of it upon your father, by charging him with the most false and devilish untruths ...

Freeman's evidence before the justices had bitten deep, and Sir George admonished his son at great length. He was in no doubt as to the true reason behind the crime, '... the main thing that provoked thee, was thy envy at thy brother's virtues and growing goodness, and that he was the elder, and that I and the world began to look on him, and love him.'

Sir George had written to the sheriff to allow Freeman a few more days to give him more time for repentance, although the main reason might have been to quell some scandalous gossip that was being spread by a former servant to the effect that the family did not carry out their religious observances.

When Freeman heard of his stay of execution to 21 August, he wrote to his 'dear and ever honoured father' begging his pardon and forgiveness of past disobedience, promising that he would spend his remaining days in repentance and prayer. Sir George replied once more, his final letter dated the day before the execution, trusting that Freeman would be received by Christ if he truly repented, but there were doubts in his mind as to whether Freeman's repentance was genuine or just the hollow words of a frightened young man seeing the pit of Hell opening for him, '... it must come from thy own self; thy own heart must beg it, or all will be in vain ... I hope thou hast some sparks of grace in thee, though deeply buried under a world of rubbish.' He also added, 'Hell is only full of impenitent souls.'

Nowhere does Sir George admit any fault of his own save, 'Too much softness and gentleness ... you have none to accuse in this but your own wicked and envious disposition, and the devil, who had got so much power over thee as to make thee do his will.' He ended the letter, 'Your sad and ruined father'. Undoubtedly Freeman was able to take some comfort from the mere fact that his father was writing to him, and there were, scattered amongst the angry diatribes, words of forgiveness, but underneath it all there was real doubt in Sir George's mind as to whether Freeman was truly sorry, in his heart of hearts. Freeman, so his father thought, might be able to fool the visiting clergymen into believing him to be a true penitent but he would never be able to hide his true feelings from God.

Freeman spent his last few days in religious observance, and achieved a spiritual calm which enabled him to sleep soundly in his bed. On the morning of Tuesday 21 August, Freeman, clad in a black gown, rode to the place of execution, a gallows constructed on a prominent hill on the south side of Penenden Heath, about a mile and a half from the gaol. He was accompanied by two clergymen and many other gentlemen. His demeanour was reported to be that of a 'mournful penitent'. Clergyman Robert Boreman, who had ministered to Freeman in the last week of his life, addressed the crowds, speaking for more than an hour about the nature of sin, and emphasising Freeman's true penitence, since there had been some rumblings of public concern about the prisoner being given Holy Communion. Following a prayer, Freeman mounted a ladder to the scaffold, and asked the people to pray for him. As the preparations were made he continued to pray, asking God to forgive him his sins and bestow a blessing on his father. His last words were 'God's will be done' and 'Lord Receive my soul.' Freeman Sondes, aged just nineteen, was duly hanged. His body was later taken to Holy Cross Church, Bearsted for burial.

*Penenden Hearth, looking towards the high ground. (Author's collection)*

# A MIRROVR OF Mercy and Iudgement.

### OR,

An Exact true Narrative of the Life and Death of *Freeman Sonds* Esquier, Sonne to Sir *George Sonds* of *Lees Court* in *Shelwich* in Kent.

Who being about the age of 19. for Murthering his Elder Brother on Tuesday the 7th of *August*, was arraigned and condemned at *Maidstone*, Executed there on Tuesday the 21. of the same Moneth 1655.

---

*Deus vindictæ gladium Misericordiæ oleo perungit.*

James chap. 2. verse 13.

*For he shall have Judgement without mercy that hath shewed no mercy, and Mercy rejoyceth over Judgement.*

---

LONDON,

Printed for *Thomas Dring*, and are to be sold at his shop at the Signe of the *George* in *Fleetstreet*, neere *Cliffords-Inne* 1655.

*A Mirrour of Mercy and Judgement. (Author's collection)*

*The graveyard, Holy Cross Church, Bearsted. (Author's collection)*

*Holy Cross Church, Bearsted. (Author's collection)*

*Sondes Chapel, Throwley. Sir George's tomb is in the foreground. (Author's collection)*

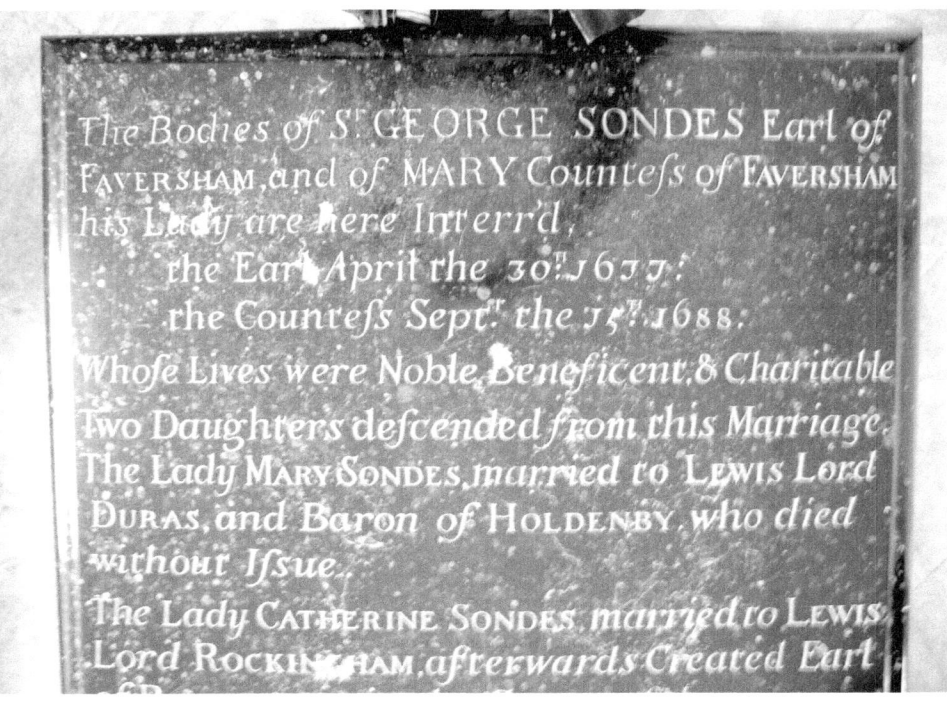

*Inscription on tomb of Sir George Sondes. (Author's collection)*

In 1656 Sir George, now fifty-seven, remarried. His object can only have been to raise a new family to which to leave his estates. His new wife was Mary Villiers who gave her age as twenty-four. Sir George soon became the father of two daughters, Mary and Katherine. The Sondes family fortunes improved with the Restoration of Charles II, and Sir George again became deputy lieutenant for Kent, and re-entered parliament in 1661. In March 1676 Lady Mary Sondes married French-born Louis de Durfort, the Marquis de Blanquerfort, and Baron Duras. A month later, Sir George was granted the titles of Baron Throwley, Viscount Sondes of Lees Court, and Earl of Feversham. Since he had no son, the titles were to revert to his son-in-law. Sir George died in 1677, and Louis succeeded to the Earldom, but the marriage remained childless, and when he died in 1709 the Earldom became extinct although the other titles were recovered by the Earl of Rockingham, Katherine's husband. Sir George could never have imagined when he raised his two sons, that the titles and the estates of the Sondes family would eventually be maintained through the female and not the male line.

The current Lees Court is not the original, which was destroyed by fire in 1910. It was rebuilt, and later sold and converted into apartments.

# 2

# DEAD OF NIGHT

## *Chislehurst, 1813*

Thomson Bonar, born in 1743 was descended from a distinguished Scottish family, a branch of which had settled in Kent. He married his first cousin Anne Thomson, eleven years his junior, and the couple had two sons and a daughter. Bonar, a wealthy merchant with trading connections in Russia, acquired the lands of Camden and Elmstead, and the magnificent Camden Place, near Chislehurst, in 1805. The Bonars were well respected in the neighbourhood, as might have been the case with any persons of substance, but they were also genuinely liked and admired, being especially noted for their gentle natures, kindness and hospitality. Thomson and Anne were a devoted couple, and despite the difference in their ages, often expressed the wish that when the time came, they would want to leave the world together.

*Camden Place. (Author's collection)*

In 1813 Bonar was seventy years of age, yet the time when he and his wife might depart their lives seemed far away, for his 'manly athletic person' was powerfully built. On Sunday 31 May he retired to bed at around midnight and Anne Bonar, as was usual, followed him at 2 a.m., asking her maid, Mary Clarke, to call her at 7. The Bonars slept in twin beds which were placed very close together. In keeping with the nightly routine, Mary lit a rushlight and placed it in the ante-room to the Bonars' bedroom, then left the doors of the ante-room and bedroom wide open.

All was quiet throughout the night, and then early in the morning those servants who lived nearby started to arrive. These early arrivals awoke the house servants whose duties required them to rise early, and they in turn were responsible for waking up those who rose later. A washerwoman was the first to arrive at her usual time of 4 a.m. and let herself in, noticing nothing untoward. Charles King, a labourer, slept at nearby Green Lane, and came to work between 5 and 6 a.m., entering the house at about twenty past six. He noticed that the front door was open, and went to wake the footman Phillip Nicholson, the only male servant who slept in the house. 'How is it you sleep with the door and window-shutters open?' demanded King. Sleepily, Nicholson replied that he didn't know they were open.

Mary Clarke shared a room with Susannah Curnick, the housemaid, who usually rose at half past six. On passing through the hall that Monday morning Susannah saw that the front door was half open. She closed it then checked the door which gave access to the lawn. This was closed, although the shutters were open. Surprised, and not a little alarmed at the thought that there may have been intruders during the night, Susannah went around checking the other doors and windows, and found

*Old Cottages in Chislehurst. (Author's collection)*

a window open in the drawing room. Going upstairs to check on the Bonars, she found the ante-room door was closed and locked, with the key outside. She opened it, and saw reddish-brown footmarks on the floor. The rushlight had gone.

Susannah, dreading the worst, dared not go in, and hurried to wake Mary Clarke, asking if she had lit the rushlight as usual and if the ante-room door had been locked. She added that there was a bad smell coming from the bedchamber. Mary knew at once that something was very wrong, and in great agitation cried out, 'Then my master and mistress are murdered!' Mary hurried to the ante-room where she looked at the footmarks and thought they were made in blood. Through the door of the bedroom she saw articles had been thrown onto the floor as if in a struggle. She too dared not enter the room but went to the wash house and got Penelope Folds, the laundry maid who had been awake since the washerwoman's arrival, and asked her to go back with her, as she was afraid that something was wrong.

Penelope and Mary went upstairs together, and while Mary cowered at the door of the Bonars' bedroom, Penelope went in and opened one of the window shutters, letting the morning light flood into the room. She turned towards the beds, clapped her hands together, and screamed. Mary had seen enough. She turned and ran downstairs to the servants' hall.

Both the Bonars had suffered repeated and powerful blows to the head with a heavy instrument. Mr Bonar lay on the floor, his head and hands covered in blood, his mouth swollen, his skull shattered into several pieces, his arms brutally mangled showing he had raised them in defence against the vicious onslaught. On the floor were pools of blood and brain matter. Locks of his grey hair were glued to his pillow and bedclothes by drying blood. The old man had obviously put up a brave and sustained fight against his murderer. Mrs Bonar, who was still in bed, had suffered a similar attack, though she seemed not to have struggled. 'There was a calm softness in her countenance more resembling a healthy sleep than a violent death.' A bent bloodstained poker was found lying on the bedroom floor, and the narrow gap between the two beds 'was almost a stream of blood.'

Randall the coachman slept over the stables. At half past seven he came into the house and was with Nicholson in the servants' hall when they heard the female servants crying 'murder!' Nicholson, 'with evident signs of perturbation and horror in his countenance' went upstairs to the room where the bodies lay. It was obvious that Mr Bonar was dead, and he covered the body with a blanket, but as Nicholson bent over Mrs Bonar he realised that she was still breathing and needed medical help. As the only male house servant it was not surprising that he at once took charge of the situation, although his next actions caused some comment. The other servants were unwilling to touch anything but Nicholson quickly stripped the bloodied sheets from his master's bed and used them to clean up the mess on the floor. He then went downstairs to the servants' hall, still holding the bundle of bloody linen, and told Mary, 'Mrs Clarke, go to your mistress, she is still alive, perhaps she may be recovered.' Pulling a clean sheet from his own bed, he used it to wrap the stained linen.

Mary ran upstairs, finding Mr Bonar's body covered in a blanket, and her mistress in bed still breathing. There was nothing she could do. A groom was sent to Bromley to get a doctor. The servants were in a state of confusion and terror, but two things at least were clear. The open doors suggested that the murder was the work of an intruder. It was also obvious from the appearance of the bedroom that the culprit must have been liberally spattered with blood, but none of the house servants had any trace of blood on their clothing. There was one suggestive piece of evidence, a bloody footmark which appeared on the stairs which connected the servants' quarters to the Bonars' room.

Although a doctor was on his way, Nicholson insisted he must go to London to fetch the noted surgeon Mr Astley Cooper to attend his mistress. The coachman eventually went with him to the stable where Nicholson took the best horse and set off at speed. On the way he paused three times for refreshments, on each occasion ordering a glass of rum for himself and a pint of porter for the horse; nevertheless he completed the journey in forty minutes, and after notifying Cooper, rode away.

Cooper travelled in haste to Chislehurst, but on examining the stricken woman declared that there was no hope. A watch was kept on Anne Bonar in case she should recover sufficiently to speak, but she only uttered two words, 'Oh! Dear!' before expiring shortly after 1 p.m. The local surgeon, Thomas Ilott, examined the body of Mr Bonar and found the skull fractured, teeth broken and jaw loosened. He had no doubt that the poker was the weapon.

*Chislehurst Common. (Author's collection)*

As the news spread throughout the neighbourhood, friends of the Bonars, local men of importance, came to the house to co-ordinate arrangements. They included the politician John Angerstein junior, son of a Russian-born merchant. Another gentleman, Mr Smith, came over on the morning of the murder, and saw the bodies and bent poker. He then went to the servants' hall, and found a bundle, which he opened. It was the bundle of sheets which Nicholson had left behind. Examining the contents he found two bloody sheets, one of fine material and the other coarse, which was the most bloody of the two. They were wrapped in a third, which was scarcely stained. He gave the two bloody sheets to a servant called Sweetapple, to take to Mr Bonar's room.

The younger Bonar son, Henry, was abroad on business, but the elder, Thomson junior, had been in Faversham on duty as colonel of the Kent militia. Having been notified of the tragedy he arrived home at 7 p.m. in a state of great distress, saying, 'let me see my father: indeed I must see him!' Despite the efforts of Mr Angerstein and the other gentlemen, he could not be prevented from rushing upstairs to look at the bodies. Bursting into the bedchamber he at once locked the door after him, to the great consternation of everyone in the house. After a period of silence from the room, the agitated onlookers ordered that the door should be broken open, and to their great relief, found Thomson junior kneeling with clasped hands over the body of his father. His friends seized hold of him, and he was taken, tottering and fainting, to another room.

Nicholson had not yet returned, but it was soon known that he had reported the murder to the police while in London, for later that day a Bow Street officer called Lavender arrived at the house. He examined the poker, which was undoubtedly the murder weapon, and was told that that it did not belong to the household, every other poker in the house being of a different design and in its proper place. He questioned the servants, but none of them had heard anything during the night. This was not entirely surprising as Camden Place is a very substantial property and the servants had slept in an area far from the wing occupied by the Bonars. When told that Nicholson had removed the sheets from the Bonars' bedroom, Lavender began to entertain suspicions of the footman, and made further searches. Finding two shoes by Nicholson's bed, he compared them with the bloody footprints in the ante-room, and felt sure that they were a match. He also found a nightcap in Nicholson's room with stains which he thought were blood. By 8 o'clock in the evening, Nicholson had not returned home, and a warrant was issued to apprehend him.

After Philip Nicholson left Mr Cooper that morning, he had not gone directly to the police but had instead looked for a man called Dale who had once been a butler at Camden Place. Only a fortnight earlier, Dale had been dismissed for bad conduct. Mrs Bonar had wanted to have him prosecuted but her husband had decided to simply send him away. Nicholson knew that Dale was a regular at the Red Lion Inn, Bishopsgate, and found him there. He told Dale about the murder, saying, 'The deed is done, and you are suspected: but you are not in it.' Only then did Nicholson go to the police office at Bow Street to give information about the murder and mention that he had seen Dale at the Red Lion. Dale at once became a suspect and officers proceeded to the Red Lion, and took him into custody. Dale was brought before the magistrates and questioned, but was able to prove that he had been at the Red Lion from eleven on Sunday evening to six on Monday morning. He was released without charge.

In Chislehurst news of the deaths brought shock and grief to the whole neighbourhood. 'There is not a man to whom a more generally favourable testimony could be borne,' stated the *Newgate Calendar*. 'Both he and his lady died regretted by all ranks in the vicinity of their residence.' The bodies were buried at St Nicholas' parish church after a solemn procession around part of the heath attended by many eminent people, including merchant John Julius Angerstein and his son.

As the day progressed, and suspicions hardened, Philip Nicholson's strange behaviour came under closer scrutiny. Had he acted from distraction due to shock or could there have been another explanation? A City officer called Forrester eventually traced Nicholson to Whitechapel, finding him on horseback, drinking at the inn door of the Three Nuns. He was 'in a state of intoxication approaching to insanity.' Forrester grabbed the bridle and, after a scuffle, secured his man, and took him to Giltspur Street Compter, a small lockup usually occupied by debtors. Questioned by Alderman Sir Charles Flower and Mr Astley Cooper, Nicholson was so drunk that it was impossible to get a statement from him. Later that day he was brought to the Mansion House to be questioned by the Lord Mayor, but he was still incoherent, and was remanded for another day.

*The Bonar Memorial, St Nicholas' Church, Chislehurst. (Author's collection)*

*St Nicholas' Church, Chislehurst. (Author's collection)*

On Tuesday he had sobered up enough to be questioned, and it was clear that it was his agitated behaviour, and 'imprudent and unfeeling manner', that had aroused suspicion rather than any firm evidence against him. Nicholson said he was the only male servant to sleep in the house. He had gone to bed at midnight on the Sunday and knew nothing about the murder until awoken the next morning. He said he had taken the sheets off the bed to clean up the mess because 'so horrid and unpleasant a sight would have been offensive to any person having occasion to enter the room.' Nicholson was taken to a private room where he was stripped and searched to see if there were any bruises on him which might have been received in the struggle with his master. A few bruises were found, the most notable being one on his forehead, but he said this had been received during his scuffle with Forrester. The officer was brought in to look at the wound and admitted that it had probably been received in that way.

After questioning, Nicholson was taken to Chislehurst to give evidence at the inquest, which took place at Camden Place commencing at 6 o'clock that evening. There being no secure lockup in the house he was briefly held in the butler's pantry before being brought before Mr Martyr, the coroner. The jury, led by foreman Mr Reeves, were sworn in and inspected the bodies before examining the witnesses.

Philip Nicholson was twenty-nine years of age and born near Belfast to a Protestant father and a Catholic mother. He was 'a man about the middle height, but bulky, well fixed and muscular.' He was said to have been involved in the Irish Rebellion of 1798 though he would have been only fourteen or fifteen at the time. Afterwards, he enlisted in the 12th Dragoons, and must have made a favourable impression as he was chosen to be servant to an officer. After being wounded in action he was discharged in January 1813, and was awarded a pension of 9$d$ a day. He obtained a position as a servant in London and later took the post of footman in the Bonars' household, where he had been working for only three weeks prior to the murder.

Under questioning, Nicholson admitted that the shoes found by his bed were his and said he thought the bloodstains had got on them when he had entered the Bonars' bedroom, but it was pointed out that the stains in the ante-room had been seen before he came up to the room.

The inquest went on until late, and just as it was drawing to a close Nicholson asked the officers guarding him if he might go into the yard to relieve himself. They refused but agreed that he could go into a water-closet, and he did so accompanied by two men. Before they could prevent him he took a razor from his pocket and cut his throat. (It was later found that he had managed to pocket the razor while held in the butler's pantry.) There was immediate consternation, and the officers trying to staunch the profusely bleeding wound at once sent for the surgeons, Mr Roberts and Mr Holt of Bromley, who had attended the inquest. It was a deep wound, and Holt ran forward, seized the gushing arteries in his hands, and stopped the flow of blood. As he did so, Roberts fought to close the wound and get the bleeding under control. An express messenger was sent to Astley Cooper, who did not arrive for another three hours.

Any lingering doubts about the prisoner's guilt had vanished, and as the doctors battled to save him, the jury returned a verdict of wilful murder against Philip Nicholson. The main concern of the court was that if he died, it would prevent the vengeance of the law from taking place.

Eventually Cooper announced that he believed the man would recover. By Wednesday evening Nicholson was able to speak but said very little, except to continue to declare his innocence of the murders when questioned by Mr Angerstein junior. He seemed calm but there was a fixedness and determination in his expression which led observers to believe that he would make another attempt on his life. He was therefore placed in a strait-waistcoat, and his arms were held by two men, one on each side. His head was also held in a steady posture to prevent any movement which might have re-opened the wound. A Bow Street officer and servants were posted to watch over him constantly.

On Monday 7 June Nicholson was visited by a number of people including Lord Camden, who was Lord of the Manor of Chislehurst; Lord Robert Seymour, a Middlesex JP with an interest in the regulation of private madhouses; and Lord Castlereagh, the Dublin-born Foreign Secretary and Leader of the House of

Commons, who would also cut his throat but more successfully in 1822. These visits, which were probably aimed at extracting a confession, made Nicholson extremely agitated, and this, together with the attempts to clean the wound before the distinguished gentlemen saw him, caused the cut to open and bleed so alarmingly that an express messenger was sent for Mr Astley Cooper. This happened at seven o'clock in the evening and Cooper arrived at eleven o' clock. A priest, Mr Bramston, and Mr Bonar junior also arrived, presumably to hear any dying words. The wound was dressed, and Nicholson appeared calm. The following morning at half past six Mr Bramston visited again, and this time Nicholson asked for Mr Bonar junior to be brought to him. On Bonar's arrival Nicholson burst into tears and said he wanted to confess to the murders. Mr Wells, the magistrate who lived at Brickley House, was sent for, and Nicholson made a full confession which he afterwards signed.

Nicholson said that on the Sunday night he had fallen asleep on a form in the servants' hall, and at three o' clock he had awoken suddenly by falling off the form. He had instantly been seized with the idea of murdering his master and mistress. Where the idea had come from he could not say. He denied that he had any motive, but the urge had been irresistible. At the time he was half undressed, but he had thrown off his waistcoat, and pulled a sheet from the bed with which he wrapped himself up. The main purpose of the sheet was disguise, but he may also have thought it would protect his clothes from blood spatter. He then took a poker from the grate of the servants' hall and rushed upstairs to his master's room. Going to his mistress's bed he struck the sleeping woman two blows on the head. She neither spoke nor moved. He then went to his master's bed, and struck him across the face. Bonar was made of strong stuff; the blow awoke him, but he was so disoriented and confused that he thought his wife was by him and said, 'Come to bed, my love'. Nicholson struck him again, but to his astonishment Bonar leaped out of bed and a struggle went on for some fifteen minutes, during which the footman thought at one point he would lose. Loss of blood eventually weakened his master who was finally overpowered, and Nicholson left the room, leaving the old man groaning on the floor. He took the rushlight to light his way downstairs, and as he descended saw that his clothes were bloodied.

In the servants' quarters he stripped naked and washed himself all over with a sponge at the sink in the butler's pantry. He then went and opened the drawing-room window so it would be thought that someone had entered the house. His shirt and stockings were covered in blood, and he took them out of the front door and hid them in a bush only a few yards outside. He returned without closing the door. The rushlight was thrown into the coal closet, so when back in his room he opened the window shutters to let in the light and went back to bed. It was not yet four o' clock. He was unable to sleep but pretended to be sleeping when King came to wake him.

He then realised that in the struggle he had dropped his bed sheet in the Bonars' room. Being of a coarser weave than his master's it would immediately point the finger of suspicion at one of the servants. He thus contrived an excuse to bundle up his own and his master's sheet together and then take them down to the servants' hall and wrap them in a sheet from his bed.

Nicholson denied he had any associate in the murder, it was not possible, 'when never in his life before to the moment of his jumping up from the form, entertained the thought of murder.' He said he had no motive for what he did, for he had no enmity or ill-will of any kind towards Mr or Mrs Bonar.

Nicholson had looked gloomy and fierce when he began his statement but by the time he had finished appeared calm, with an expression of satisfaction about his face. A search was made for the hidden clothing, which was found in a laurel bush close to the house. The stockings were very bloody, and the shirt demonstrated what a fierce struggle had taken place, for it was torn almost to rags at the neck and front.

Slowly, Nicholson recovered from his terrible injuries, but was not able to give any details of the crime beyond what he had already stated. There was considerable public speculation as to his motives, and Thomson Bonar junior became increasingly obsessed with discovering what had driven Nicholson to murder his parents.

It was known that the footman had complained about his mistress getting the carriage out often which required him to follow behind it, and it was speculated that this, though trivial, might have been a source of ill-will. He had also been seen drinking a great deal of beer on the Sunday prior to the crime, and it was suggested that this might have had some effect on his senses.

A few days before the murder, Nicholson had called at the tavern of Mr Munro in Jews Row, Chelsea. There he met with his father, Patrick, handed him some clothes and roast beef, and settled his bill. The conversation turned to the Roman Catholic Relief Bill, designed to reduce the legal restrictions on activities of Catholics, which had failed to become law in the House of Commons on 24 May, and Nicholson cursed all those who opposed it. It was alleged that Mr Bonar had later expressed his satisfaction at the failure of the Bill while Nicholson was waiting at table, and that the murder had been motivated by revenge. This rumour was denied by Bonar's friends, who said it was most improbable 'from the known conciliatory and tolerant character of the deceased gentleman,' that Mr Bonar had expressed himself in such a way.

On 17 August Nicholson made his will, leaving his clothes to his father, together with £4 'to defray his expenses home to Ireland.' All the remainder of his effects were bequeathed to his mother, Bridget.

The trial took place at the Maidstone Assizes on Friday 20 August, and as might have been expected, the court was packed within minutes of the doors being opened. Mr Justice Heath was at the bench at eight o' clock and Nicholson was at once brought to the bar. He seemed composed, but gloomy. He was charged not with murder but petty treason, since the indictment was for traitorously and feloniously killing his master, an act of betrayal considered to be worse than common murder. His manner throughout the trial was 'more sorry and ashamed than agitated: his face is of a feeble cast: his manner was at once dejected and firm.'

*An Account of the Life, Trial, Confession, and Dying Words of Philip Nicholson. (Author's collection)*

One mystery was solved. The poker had, after all, come from the Bonars' house. It had not been recognised initially because it was not the one mainly used at the servants' hall, but a second one, lighter and more portable than the first.

Questioned by Mr Bonar junior as to whether he had accomplices, Nicholson answered simply: 'No, Sir, I would tell you if I had.' He confirmed that Dale the butler and the other servants knew nothing of his intentions. Asked for his motive he replied, 'I had no bad intention: I did not know what provoked me to do it, more than you do.'

Only one witness was called to testify to the previous good character of the prisoner. Mr Frederick Tyrrell said he was the son of the City remembrancer, an officer who assisted the Lord Mayor. Nicholson had lived with Tyrrell's father for three years, and 'his conduct during that time was humane and gentle: he appeared to be a man of a kind disposition.' Unfortunately the witness revealed in cross-examination that Nicholson had been dismissed for drunkenness. He had never been violent, but it had been considered unsafe to retain him because of the risks in handling lights. Tyrrell admitted that he had often seen Nicholson drunk, though not outrageously so.

Mr Justice Heath summed up, saying that he had never seen a case so clearly proven, and the jury almost immediately returned a verdict of guilty. In passing sentence the judge expressed the general feeling of bewilderment at why the crime had happened at all. 'What was your motive for so atrocious a crime does not appear: it does not seem to have been revenge; you were not intoxicated, nor offended at your master, against whom it was impossible to feel resentment, for his whole life was a series of kindness and beneficences ...' Nicholson was sentenced to be hanged, and his body 'given to be dissected and anatomized.' Nicholson listened to the dread sentence with an air more of sorrow than fear. He then offered a paper which he asked to have read out in court. The judge said that this was most irregular but after looking at the paper gave permission for it to be read.

In the document, Nicholson, with deep contrition, acknowledged his sole guilt of the crime, and implored forgiveness of his master's family:

> I myself had no intention of committing these horrid deeds, save for a short time, so short as scarcely to be computed before I actually committed them: that booty was not the motive of my fatal cruelties; I am sure the idea of plunder never presented itself to my mind: I can attribute those unnatural murders to no other cause than, at the time of their commission, a temporary fury from excessive drinking; and before that time to the habitual forgetfulness, for many years, of the Great God and his judgements; and the too natural consequence of such forgetfulness, the habitual yielding to the worst passions of corrupted nature ...

Nicholson was taken to the condemned cell in Maidstone Gaol, which 'is under ground, and the approach to it is dark and dreary, down many steps.' Here, at half past five on the following Monday morning, Thomson Bonar junior went to speak to the condemned man. He met with him once more at twelve o' clock, together with his brother and Mr Bramston. Soon afterwards, a hurdle in the shape of a shallow box 6ft by 3ft was drawn up to the door of the gaol. At each end was a seat just capable of holding two people. Nicholson, double-ironed, was placed in the vehicle with his back to the horses. He was pinioned with ropes, and the rope with which he was to be hanged was coiled about his shoulders. The executioner sat beside him, and in the seats opposite sat Mr Bramston and one of the jailers armed with a loaded blunderbuss.

At Penenden Heath, a gallows had recently been built in the new style. The old method of execution was for the condemned person with the noose around his neck to be placed in a cart which would be driven away to leave him dangling. The new gallows was a platform raised 7ft above the ground. It had a drop through which the condemned person would plunge, and there was room enough to hang about a dozen people at once. The hurdle arrived just before 2 p.m., and stopped underneath the gallows, where an immense crowd had assembled to watch the execution. There was a pause for Bramston and Nicholson to kneel in prayer. Thomson Bonar junior was already there, some 12yds from the gallows in his post-chaise. The side windows were covered with blinds but the front, which faced the gallows, was open.

Nicholson ascended by a ladder. He was calm, and his step was firm. All morning he had been asked how he felt and he had replied that he had never felt so comfortable since he committed the crime. He believed he had made his peace with God, and said that he was so satisfied to die that if a free pardon was offered him he would rather die than accept it.

Bonar, determined to wring from the prisoner the motive for the murders, deputed someone to climb up to the platform after the rope was placed around Nicholson's neck and demand from him whether it was true that he had no accomplice and no motive. Nicholson was adamant that he had no accomplices and, clasping his hands

*Penenden Heath pictured from the high ground. (Author's collection)*

together, said, 'As God is in heaven, it was a momentary thought, as I have repeatedly declared before.'

Soon afterwards the drop opened and Nicholson fell to his doom. Calculation of the length of the drop was then a primitive concept, and despite the fall his neck did not break at once, and he died hard, greatly convulsed. The body hung for an hour and was then put in a post-chaise and taken to Bromley for burial.

Executions continued to be carried out at Penenden Heath until 1830, the last such being commemorated by a slab in the churchyard of Holy Cross Church, Bearsted.

Why did Nicholson commit the murders? He was clearly sane, thinking clearly and well aware of what he was doing. The use of the sheet as a disguise before he even entered the Bonars' bedroom shows premeditation, and his concealment of the incriminating sheet and bloodstained clothes demonstrate that he knew he had committed an act which was against the law. Nowadays it might be suggested that excessive alcohol plus the shock of sudden awakening when he fell from the form had brought on a fit of temporary insanity. In 1813, however, the gallows was the only possible outcome.

*The slab at Holy Cross Church, Bearsted, commemorating the last execution to be carried out at Penenden Heath. (Author's collection)*

# 3

# THE SAVIOUR OF THE PEOPLE

## *Canterbury, 1838*

In 1832 the city of Canterbury was a busy trading centre with 15,000 inhabitants, surrounded by orchards, hop gardens and ancient woods. Kent is often referred to as 'the garden of England' yet political and social discontent simmered violently beneath the face of the beautiful land, frequently erupting into outright demonstrations of unrest. It was the humble labourer burdened by the demands of rents and tithes whose livelihood was most under threat to the whims of weather and economic change. When threshing machines were introduced in 1830, thus reducing opportunities for employment, the labourers of East Kent embarked on a tour of destruction, smashing the machines and setting fire to farmhouses. There was no regular county police force, and the villagers were so terrified that troops had to be called out to patrol the lanes at night.

These lawless uprisings were the labourers' only means of protest. Only freemen of the city, a status conferred by birth, position or purchase, were empowered to vote at municipal and parliamentary elections, and abuse of power, selling of votes, and outright bribery were commonplace. Canterbury elections frequently led to scenes of destructive unrest which could only be quelled by the appointment of special constables. The Archbishop of Canterbury himself was known to be against electoral reform and on his visit to the city in August 1832 his carriage was surrounded by noisy protesters. After dining at the Guildhall, he departed for the Cathedral in his carriage, which was pelted with every kind of missile the mob could lay its hands on.

These spontaneous demonstrations lacked one thing that would give them a concentrated driving force – a charismatic and powerful leader, someone who would focus the people's discontent and make turbulence explode into a frenzy in which they would act without heed of personal consequences. In September 1832 that leader arrived.

He was a remarkable looking figure. By the standards of the day he was a giant of a man, almost 6ft in height, broad, and deep chested, with powerful, well-muscled arms. His face was swarthily handsome, the eyes a brilliant blue with a piercing intense stare. Long black hair fell to his shoulders, and he sported an impressive bushy beard, of which he was obviously proud, taking care that it was shiny and well groomed. His garments were rich, colourful and exotic. Such a figure might well provoke alarm or distrust, and indeed his look was so strange that the landlord of the Fountain Inn refused to accommodate him, and he was obliged to take a room at the Rose Inn. He called himself Count Moses Rostopchein Rothschild, and his mission was to become famous.

To achieve this it was only necessary to walk around the streets of Canterbury in his extraordinary attire, bestowing peppermints on the children, charming the women, buying rounds of drink in public houses, and letting everyone infer that he was a man of wealth who believed in helping the poor. To some individuals he revealed that he was able to invest funds which could pay out handsome interest, and not a few dupes handed over their hard-earned money to him, including Thomas Stroud, a waiter at the Rose Inn.

After a few weeks, however, Count Moses Rothschild decided that he was making insufficient headway, and so, quite abruptly, he changed not only his name but his identity.

He now proclaimed himself to be Sir William Percy Honywood Courtenay, Knight of Malta, heir to the Earldom of Devon, and the estate of Hales Place, which lay just north of Canterbury. He was also, of course, King of the Gypsies and King of Jerusalem. So natural to him was the change of persona that it seems to have been accepted by the population without comment, indeed they liked his second incarnation much better than his first, and he began to increase the numbers of his admirers.

No one challenged his claims, least of all the real Earl of Devon, who was obliged to live abroad to avoid being charged with offences 'of so odious a nature' they could not be named. The sixth Baronet Hales had died without issue in 1829, and Sir John Courtenay Honywood, to whom Sir William presumably claimed kinship, had died in September 1832. It was later claimed that Sir William had purchased some of Sir John's effects, including a fine sword and ceremonial epaulettes, to add to the impressiveness of his costume. Despite being refused permission to enter Hales Place, Sir William, in his new accoutrements, cut a convincing figure.

In December 1832 the first general election under the terms of the new Parliamentary Reform Act, under which copyholders and leaseholders were permitted to vote, was to take place. A strong reform movement in Canterbury eagerly expected the return of the two Whig candidates, and the Tories felt so sure of defeat that they did not plan to put up a candidate. It was then suggested that the new man of the people, Sir William Courtenay, should be asked to stand, if only

Sir William Percy Honywood Courtenay. (Author's collection)

because it would cost the Whigs far more trouble and expense than an uncontested election. Sir William at once agreed to stand as an Independent, and, claiming to be 'the Heir of that family which none in Europe can excel', published an address to the voters of Canterbury, in which he urged them to elect:

> ... those only that will boldly and determinedly pledge themselves to annihilate for ever, the TITHES, taxation upon all the shopkeepers and productive classes, also upon knowledge, the primogeniture law, chartered and corporate bodies, slavery, sinecures and placemen ...

The publication was eagerly sought after. The new candidate joined some of the gentleman's clubs in the city and let it be known that he expected to come into a splendid inheritance upon which he would reward those who supported him. Dressed in flamboyant attire he drove around the city in a barouche, stopping every so often to make speeches. These diversions proved enormously popular, since his language was bold and colourful, his voice stirring, and he claimed to oppose every measure which gave discontent to his listeners. On one occasion his enthusiastic supporters insisted on pulling the barouche back to the Rose Inn themselves, and would not be satisfied until he had addressed them from the balcony. While some more cautious souls began to cast doubts on his claims to land and titles, nothing came of this since it was impossible to determine who he actually was.

The election took place in the Guildhall on 10 December with a noisy crowd filling the building and chanting support for Courtenay. Sir William, splendidly dressed in crimson velvet trimmed with gold, pledged to transfer the burden of taxation from the poor to the rich and 'promised a return to the good old days of roast beef and mutton and plenty of prime, nut brown ale ...' Voting was done by a show of hands, but to the onlookers' consternation, the people's favourite came a poor third, polling less than twenty per cent of the votes. Undeterred, Sir William made a stirring speech to his supporters, and amidst scenes of wild excitement announced that he would stand for Parliament in the election for East Kent. Returning to the Rose Inn, he addressed the cheering crowds from the balcony.

One week later thousands of people from all over the county assembled at Barham Down for the nomination of the candidates for the East Kent election. Two Tory candidates and one Whig arrived with their supporters, but the most startling figure was Sir William in black velvet trousers and vest, gold belt, silver epaulettes, crimson

*Sir William Courtenay addressing the crowd in High Street, Canterbury, from the balcony of the Rose Inn. (Author's collection)*

cap and red stockings, with incongruously large shoes to guard against the mud. To add to that curious impression, he spent the time during his rivals' speeches adopting unusual postures and making faces. Despite the support of the mob, his public performances had made him an object of amusement, and certainly not a man whom the public wished to represent them. More than 9,000 votes were cast in the election, but only three people voted for Sir William, who now had to ponder this disheartening reverse.

Over the next few weeks he toured the county and, due to his considerable entertainment value, was much in demand as a speaker. In March 1833 he launched a newspaper called the *Lion*, in which, with many expressions of religious fervour, he championed the poor of the land and attacked the government, the clergy and the aristocracy. In his efforts to court publicity, however, he was about to make a catastrophic error of judgement.

That February a fishing smack, the *Admiral Hood*, had been challenged by a Revenue cutter, *Lively*, on suspicion of smuggling. The crew of the *Admiral Hood* were seen to throw some tubs overboard which, on being recovered, were found to contain spirits. The seven crewmen were arrested and tried at Rochester on 1 March. Sir William saw this as an opportunity to make a name for himself as a supporter of the poor. Offering to conduct the defence of skipper Thomas Coltrupp, he astounded and impressed the fisherman into discharging his lawyer. Sir William's theatrical and rambling speeches cut no ice with the jury, who found Coltrupp guilty, and the remaining six sailors immediately elected to be defended by their lawyer. Disappointed, Sir William volunteered to appear as witness for the defence whereupon he testified that he had been returning to England from France on a vessel he called the *Active* when he saw tubs floating in the sea, which he was certain had not come from the *Admiral Hood*. To his astonishment, the remaining crewmen were also found guilty.

He had gone too far. On 18 March he was told that he would be prosecuted for perjury. On 28 March he was arrested on a charge of swindling Thomas Stroud out of £150. Due to the unpopularity of the mayor and Corporation of Canterbury, this temporarily worked in his favour, and violent demonstrations took place demanding Sir William's release from Westgate gaol. Eventually he was released on bail to the enthusiastic acclaim of the mob. During the course of the proceedings Sir William acquired a fervent new supporter, George Francis, a well-to-do yeoman farmer of Fairbook Farm in Boughton-under-Blean. Mr Francis was delighted to welcome Sir William to his home, where he listened avidly to his new guest's religious and political outpourings.

Sir William finally appeared in court on 1 July at the Guildhall, Canterbury, which was crowded with noisy demonstrators. 'All order, all decorum, all regard to common decency were alike set at defiance by the deluded followers of this mountebank impostor,' said the *Kent Herald* in disgust. Charged with obtaining money under false pretences he was remanded to await trial on the more serious charge of perjury. The trial took place at Maidstone on 25 July.

Evidence was produced that at the time when Sir William claimed to have seen the tubs floating in the sea he had actually been in church at Boughton-under-Blean. To his astonishment, he was found guilty and sentenced to imprisonment for three months after which he would be transported for the term of seven years.

Languishing in Maidstone Gaol, still insisting that he was descended from the best blood in England, and would soon be able to prove it, his years of imposture were about to catch up with him. A spectator at his trial had observed a similarity between the distinctive Sir William Courtenay and a John Nichols Tom, who had gone missing in May 1832 and whose relatives had been advertising for information. Before long, the Tom family had been contacted and Mrs Catherine Tom arrived in Maidstone and identified the prisoner as her husband.

John Nichols Tom was born in St Colomb, Cornwall in 1799, the son of William Tom, an innkeeper and maltster. John Tom was a spirited and mischievous boy, with a strong dislike of authority. Expelled from his first school, he was sent to a private school where it was hoped he would be under firmer control. There, he listened daily to the powerful sermons of the Revd Richard Cope, and was impressed both by his religious fervour and the power of dramatic speeches to sway his listeners. Gifted with a highly retentive memory, Tom was given to conceited and pompous displays of learning, and found it hard to concentrate on any profession. After trying a number of occupations he became a clerk to a firm of wine merchants. He married Catherine Fulpitt in 1821 and in 1827 he took over the wine merchants' business on the retirement of the partners, adding the trade of malting. During these years he showed no signs of any wish to promote himself as a leader of men, although he was given to lecturing anyone who would listen on his religious and political beliefs. Two terrible shocks may have helped to upset his mental balance. In 1827 his mother, Charity, who had been showing signs of insanity, was removed to an asylum where she later died. In the following year his business premises burned down. He was able to rebuild, but in 1829 he started behaving eccentrically. In 1830 his mind gave way and he was unable to attend to his business, but in the following year he was sufficiently recovered to recommence trading. In December 1831 he again showed symptoms of insanity and received treatment from a surgeon for two months. Apparently recovered, in May 1832 he departed on a business trip to Liverpool, taking malt to sell. He wrote to his wife on 3 May saying he had just sold the malt and would write to her again in a day or two. The second letter never arrived. John Nichols Tom had vanished.

It is probable that he spent several months in London posing as a country squire, and after meeting some rabbis, allowed his hair and beard to grow and took on the name Count Rothschild. He left London, possibly due to lack of funds, and in September 1832 he arrived in Canterbury.

Once Mrs Tom revealed the unfortunate history of her husband it was agreed that Sir William, for so he continued to be called, was insane, and ought to be transferred to an asylum rather than be transported. On 28 October he was admitted to the Kent County Lunatic Asylum, Barming Heath. Despite this, there were many who still supported him, including Mr Francis, who made applications to have him released. The medical superintendent, Mr Poynder, confirmed that his patient conducted himself in a peaceful and orderly fashion but added, 'though I believe he himself would harm no one, I cannot answer for the conduct of others, who might be excited by his unsound and extravagant opinions.'

By 1837, however, Sir William's continued good behaviour encouraged the belief that it would be safe to place him in the care of his family, who were eager for his release. His father consulted Sir Hussey Vivian, a distinguished Truro man elected to parliament in the August of that year, who approached Lord John Russell the Home Secretary on the family's behalf. On the understanding that the patient would return to Cornwall in the care of his father, the Home Secretary advised the young Queen Victoria to sign a free pardon for Courtenay.

The only difficulty was that the patient continued to insist that he was the rightful Earl of Devon. He refused to acknowledge his wife and father and had no intention of going back to Cornwall. To ensure his son's release, William Tom had to find another person willing to take charge of him. That man was George Francis, 'a person of small understanding and little education, but of great pride and insatiable vanity' according to the Revd Handley of Hernhill, who knew him well. Dazzled by Sir William's confident claims and impressive manners, enthralled by his religious devotion, and believing that when his guest finally proved his claims to the titles and lands he called his own he would enjoy prestige and financial rewards, Francis was all too eager to attach himself to Sir William Courtenay. He refused to believe that Sir William was married, and may well have hoped to welcome a title into his own family as he had an eligible daughter.

At the end of October 1837 Sir William Courtenay emerged from the asylum where he had spent four years, and looked for opportunities. They were not hard to find, and as ever he saw the discontented poor as his potential disciples. In 1834 the Whig government had enacted the Poor Law Amendment Act. Prior to that, the wages of poorly paid labourers were supplemented by the rates, but that relief was now abolished, and those unable to work were obliged to enter a workhouse. Labourers met to protest against the new laws, and violent disturbances followed. Heavy prison sentences meted out to the rioters had subdued the outbreaks, but left feelings of bitter resentment. To Sir William, what these suffering people needed was a leader.

For some weeks, Sir William lived quietly with Francis and his family, behaving with perfect propriety and giving no hint that he wished to do anything other than establish his right to his professed titles and claim his property. As time passed, however, Francis saw little evidence of progress, and began to press his guest to take action, something Sir William began to find irksome. He had acquired a horse, a light grey mare on which he rode around the countryside, talking to the farmers, exerting his masculine charm over their wives and making a fuss of the children. Francis, who wished to distance himself from the lower orders of society, was horrified when he discovered that his aristocratic guest was courting the support of the local labourers. A break was inevitable, and in January 1838 when Sir William arrived at Fairbrook sporting a brace of pistols, Francis demanded he get rid of them, and when his guest refused, ordered him to leave. Unruffled, Sir William rode away on his mare, knowing he had sufficient support not to need Francis any more.

One of Sir William's most fervent devotees was Sarah Culver, a plain, forty-year-old spinster, whose parents occupied Bossenden Farm. His frequent visits brought excitement to her drab isolated life, and she was soon wholly under his sway. Her mother too was not immune from the rakish charms of the swaggering Sir William. His ability to invoke the scriptures also impressed serious souls like the deeply religious William Wills, who offered Sir William the use of his cottage not far from Fairbrook. The impressionable Wills began to believe in his visitor as both superhuman and divine, and inspired Sir William to more dangerous delusions. His lectures to the villagers took on a spiritual tone, and with his long flowing hair and Biblical beard, it was not hard to persuade the credulous people that he was the reincarnation of Jesus Christ come to earth to do away with evil. Wills embraced this concept with passionate devotion and worked hard to convert others to believe in the new incarnation of the Saviour.

Even Sir William knew that mere talk could not go on for ever. Action was needed, firm and dramatic. On Sunday 27 May 1838 he called a meeting at Dunkirk, where, surrounded by some 200 people, he read passages from the Bible about the corruption of the rich and their oppression of the poor. He then commanded his attentive and enthusiastic listeners to prepare themselves, for on the Tuesday they must leave whatever they were doing to follow him.

Sir William spent Monday at Bossenden Farm and the following morning set out with a few followers and bought bread and cheese. At Wills' cottage more supporters were waiting. After a meal of bread, cheese and beer, Sir William ordered that a loaf be placed atop a pole, which was given to one of his men, William Price, and commanded the others to follow this powerful standard. Wills was assigned the honour of bearing a banner depicting the British Lion. Sir William had doffed his usual rich clothing and wore a farmer's smock with a leather belt, into which he had stuck his pistols and a sword. This warlike appearance did not deter his disciples, as they were used to his showy manner and habit of firing his pistols into the air to make a dramatic end to his rousing speeches.

The little group marched past admiring crowds of women lining the road and after passing Fairbrook House, turned toward Faversham. Calling a sudden halt, and telling his men to wait, Sir William, Wills and three others crossed a meadow towards a stack of beansticks, where to the great discomfiture of those watching it appeared that he was trying to set them alight. This effort failed, however, and he returned, declaiming, 'I am now going to strike the bloody blow! The streets that have heretofore flowed with water shall flow with blood for the rights of the poor!' Some of his followers, realising that the escapade might develop from a pleasant stroll with free food and drink into something illegal and dangerous, took the opportunity to slip away.

The party next called at the home of Mrs Hadlow, William Wills' sister, who was an ardent supporter, and then marched on via Goodnestone, Graveney and Dargate Common trying to recruit others as they went, returning footsore and weary to Bossenden Farm, where Sarah Culver and her mother provided a meal. Despite his efforts Sir William had still only about twenty followers, but undeterred, he told his exhausted men that they must be up early the next day, when new recruits would join them and their cause would be victorious.

One thing that Sir William had not taken into account when asking men to down tools and join him was that the labourers whose support he needed were not free agents. Mr Curling, a farmer of Hernhill, came to Bossenden and an angry exchange took place. Curling said that four of his labourers had joined Sir William and he demanded they return, since not only were their wives anxious about them, but the men had broken their contract with him. Getting no satisfaction Curling hurried away to complain to a justice of the peace.

He was not the only person to be concerned. Earlier that day Col. Groves, of Boughton, had informed Dr Poore, a Sittingbourne JP, of the rumours that Sir William was gathering a potentially violent mob, and that evening George Francis came to tell Poore of the rabble-rousing speech made on Sunday, and how the men had departed in martial style that very morning. Poore, anxious to gather as much information as possible, contacted Mr Poynder of Barming Lunatic Asylum, and was concerned to discover that Poynder believed Sir William still to have been of unsound mind when released.

On the Wednesday morning Sir William and his men were up at 3 a.m. Four hours later they arrived at Sittingbourne and Dr Poore, hearing of their arrival with some alarm, discovered them calmly eating breakfast at the Wheatsheaf Inn. He hurried to Faversham, meeting up with Col. Groves and Mr Francis, who had been gathering more evidence. With them were Mr Curling and two of Sir William's erstwhile followers who had prudently slipped away; Alfred Payne, a harness-maker of Canterbury, and John Dunkin, a Boughton labourer. All three supplied Poore with what he needed: signed statements that Sir William had been engaged in illegal activities. Poore was now able to make out a warrant for the arrest of Sir William and his trusted lieutenants. This was passed to John Mears, the High Constable of Boughton-under-Blean.

Despite a long day's march and Sir William's rousing recruitment speeches along the way, the party of rebels finally returned to Bossenden Farm on the Wednesday evening, tired, downhearted, and very few more in number than had set out. Their leader must have known that unless something encouraging happened on the following day they whole enterprise would fragment, and he would find himself deserted by all but a devoted few.

At 4.30 a.m. on Thursday 31 May, John Mears, armed only with a staff, set out for Bossenden Farm to execute the warrant, taking with him his brother, Nicholas, and Petty Constable Daniel Edwards. Nicholas Mears, unhappy about the potential dangers, agreed to come out of loyalty to his brother but as they walked up the narrow lane to the farm his sense of foreboding increased, and he said that if anyone was to die it had better be him and not John, who had children to support. In the yard outside the farmhouse they saw two men whom they recognised, Thomas Mears, who was a relative of the brothers, and William Price, both of whom immediately gave the alert. As the three men climbed over the stile in the fence separating the road from the farmhouse, Sir William appeared with a face of thunder, and strode up to them, pausing only a few yards away.

'Are you the constable?' he demanded. When both the Mears brothers said 'Yes' Sir William took a pistol from his belt and shot Nicholas, who staggered back against the fence then fell to the ground. Sir William then drew his sword and ran at John Mears. Mears and Edwards ran for their lives towards the shelter of the woods. Fortunately for them, their pursuer stumbled, and by the time he was on his feet again they had disappeared. Sir William's rage had now exploded to the point where the small sense of restraint of which he had once been master had boiled away.

*Thomas Mears and William Price. (Author's collection)*

*The staff held by John Mears when he went to arrest Sir William. (Courtesy of Kent Police Museum)*

*The Murder of Nicholas Mears. (Author's collection)*

Seeing Mears groaning upon the ground, begging for help, he drew his sword and struck him with it three times, then pulled out the second pistol and shot him again, killing him outright.

He turned to where his followers stood staring at him, appalled at the homicidal madness that had overtaken their leader, not one of them daring to move. 'I am the Saviour of the World!' he cried. 'You are my true lambs – every one of you!' Looking down on the body of his victim he added, 'Though I have killed the body, I have saved the soul!' Unconvinced, some of the men began to back away, but Sir William brandished his blood-smeared sword, and threatened, 'If anyone tries to run away, he shall be a dead man!' No one doubted him. At their leader's order, four of them threw the body of Nicholas Mears into a ditch. The atmosphere at Bossenden Farm was one of silent terror. No one dared disobey Sir William, who ordered his men to follow him to Mrs Hadlow's house. Before he left, he told the still besotted Sarah Culver that if he should fall in battle she must anoint his lips with water and he would instantly recover. Having charged her with this sacred mission he strode away, his men obediently trooping after him.

Mrs Hadlow's son, Henry, was working in a nearby field, and he was ordered to ride home and tell his mother to prepare breakfast. Before he departed, however, one of the men managed to whisper to him about the murder of Nicolas Mears. Young Hadlow galloped away, and was able to pass on the news as he rode through Hernhill, but when he arrived home and told his mother, she, as an ardent devotee of Sir William, simply prepared the meal for the expected guests.

While Sir William and his frightened men were breakfasting, John Mears and Daniel Edwards had arrived at Crockham Farm, the home of Mr Curling, who, on hearing their news, departed to Canterbury to ask for soldiers to be sent to deal with the situation. Edwards and Mears went on to Faversham where the magistrate, Norton Knatchbull, issued a new warrant for the arrest of Sir William, Thomas Mears and William Price.

After breakfast, Sir William addressed his followers once more. His message was beginning to sound familiar, and the words less impressive from the mouth of a brutal murderer. As he promised to divide the estates of the rich between his men, they now had a good idea of just how he intended to deprive the rich of their property. When they looked a little doubtful he grew wilder and more impassioned, claiming to be the Christ, the resurrected Jesus, their Saviour who had come down to earth in a cloud to lead them all to Glory. No weapon could harm him, or any of his followers. Gradually his words moved them, and some of the men joyfully acknowledged him as their Saviour and vowed to follow him. Others were more hesitant and he harangued them, threatening damnation to those who did not comply. He was unexpectedly halted in mid-tirade by a passing woodcutter, who approached him, shook hands, and asked politely if it was true that he had shot Nicholas Mears. 'Yes!' cried Sir William, 'I *did* shoot the vagabond – and I have eaten a hearty breakfast since!'

The men marched on, collecting a few stragglers along the way, and by the time they reached Fairbrook, they numbered thirty-seven. The ladies of the house were prevailed upon to serve the men with beer but before they could do so George Francis arrived and, having heard about what had happened, was horrified to see the murderous gang outside his home. He demanded that Sir William leave the premises at once. What might have transpired then is unknown, but at that moment soldiers were seen approaching the farmhouse.

Norton Knatchbull had left Faversham accompanied by at least a dozen men, some of whom were civilian volunteers who had been made special constables for the emergency. One of these was nineteen-year-old George Catt, who kept a beerhouse. They were a few minute's ride from Fairbrook when they encountered Dr Poore who said that Sir William and his men were at Fairbrook, but it would be best to wait until the troops arrived before approaching. Knatchbull was keen to try and tackle Sir William himself, and ignoring Dr Poore's advice, led his men down the lane that led to the farm. It was this contingent that arrived just as George Francis was ordering Sir William to leave. Sir William told his men to follow him to some nearby osier beds where he judged there would be more room for the confrontation.

There, he taunted Knatchbull, suggesting single combat. He then spotted that Revd Handley and his brother Major Handley had ridden up behind him, separated from his forces only by a narrow stream. The Handleys, oblivious to any danger, begged some of Sir William's men, who were known to them, to abandon their desperate enterprise. This enraged Sir William, who fired his pistol at them, fortunately missing. With a blast on his bugle he summoned his men to move on, and they marched with him in the direction of Bossenden Wood. On the way, pistol shots were exchanged between Sir William and Knatchbull, which again missed their targets. While all this was happening the troops finally arrived; a hundred men and three officers of the 45th Infantry under the command of Major Armstrong. The troops met up with Knatchbull and Dr Poore at the Red Lion Inn, where they learned that the rebels had stopped at a clearing in Bossenden Wood near the footpath from Old Barn Lane.

Major Armstrong decided to divide his men into two detachments. He would lead his men down Old Barn Lane which lay north of the clearing and then take the footpath towards Sir William and his men. Meanwhile Captain Reid would take his men down the road to Bossenden Farm, which lay south of the clearing, to cut off any retreat. Dr Poore read the Riot Act and they were ready to move off. A large crowd of civilians had gathered, and Armstrong realised that they wanted to follow him and watch the show. He quickly cooled their intentions by telling them that if they did follow he would ask them to assist the soldiers. 'From the character I have heard of this man Courtenay,' he added, 'I am afraid there will be something serious happening.' As the men marched away to battle the weather, which had been hot and oppressive, erupted into a storm. Thunder and lightening banged and crackled overhead, and rain cascaded down. Most of the onlookers hurried into the Red Lion, to the great appreciation of the landlord.

Captain Reid and his fifty men moved into position without hindrance, until they came to the edge of Bossenden Wood. Reid stayed back with half of his men, but sent Lt Bennett, Norton Knatchbull and the rest of the men on ahead, into the wood itself, to get as close to Sir William as possible.

In the clearing Sir William was having problems. The wife of one of his followers, William Burford, had come to plead with him to allow her husband to return home. Sir William's reply was to threaten to shoot her if she did not leave, adding that he would shoot her husband too if he stirred a step. There was nothing the distraught woman could do but hurry away.

The weather had cleared and it was a bright and hot afternoon. Major Armstrong's men had reached the end of the footpath and were loading their weapons when Sir William spotted Lt Bennett's men, and ordered his followers to attack. Bennett, a young eager officer, strode forward, sword held aloft, demanding that Sir William surrender in the name of the Queen, but the madman, with a fixed and determined stare drew his pistol and shot him dead. Knatchbull at once took a shot at Sir William, whose followers, armed with cudgels and staves charged forward. Major Armstrong gave his men the order to fire. William Burford was shot dead and George Catt, who had rushed up ahead and been close to Bennett, was killed by the troops' fire. For a few minutes the clearing was a mass of screaming, cudgel wielding, punching and kicking men.

Sir William, the focus of much of the firepower, was hit in the chest, then a civilian volunteer, Thomas Milgate, battered him to the ground with a cudgel. Still his followers fought like demons on the trampled bloodied earth and only a massed bayonet charge finally made them turn and run. Major Armstrong at once ordered his bugler to sound the cease-fire. The battle was over.

At Bossenden Farm, Sarah Culver heard the sound of gunshots, and knew what she must do. Filling a pail with water, she hurried through the woods to the clearing, but she was intercepted and arrested by a constable before she could reach Sir William and carry out her mission.

Sir William Courtenay was dead. Seven of his men; George Branchett, William Burford, George Griggs, Edward Wraight, William Rye, William Foster, and Phineas Harvey, had been killed, and one, Stephen Baker, was close to death. The body of Lt Bennett was taken to the Red Lion and placed in a back bedroom, while the bodies of Sir William and all his followers, except Griggs, were also carried to the Red Lion and laid out in the stables. The bodies of George Catt, George Griggs, and Stephen Baker, who had succumbed before he could get medical help, were placed in the stables of the White Horse, Boughton. In the same inn, Nicholas Mears lay ready for his post-mortem. As the day went on, more of Sir William's followers were rounded up and brought to the White Horse where they were guarded by troops.

Six of the rebels had been captured in the woods, and were handcuffed together; these were Alexander Foad, John Spratt, William Wills, Edward Wraight junior, Edward Curling, and Thomas Mears. Sarah Culver, who was suspected of being an accomplice, was handcuffed to Spratt. All were removed to St Augustine's Gaol, Canterbury.

As the news spread, so sightseers and souvenir hunters descended on the Red Lion, staring at the bodies of the dead, and tearing from them fragments of bloodstained clothing. The landlord was eventually obliged to nail his doors and windows shut to prevent the invasion of his premises. The post-mortem examination of Sir William showed that he had suffered a number of cuts about the face and left arm, and there was a bloody wound on his head, but the cause of death was a bullet which had pierced his lungs.

*The tragic scene at Bossenden Wood. (Author's collection)*

During the inquests that followed, at the White Horse, a verdict of wilful murder of Nicholas Mears was brought against William Courtenay and William Burford, both of whom were dead, and four others, William Price, Thomas Mears, Alexander Foad, and William Nutting, who were committed to Maidstone Gaol. For the murder of Lt Bennett, verdicts of wilful murder were returned against Courtenay and eighteen of his followers, including Mears and Foad, although nine of those named were dead and one seriously wounded.

Lt Bennett was buried in the precincts of Canterbury Cathedral on 2 June. A tablet in his memory was later placed on the north wall of the nave.

During the magistrates' hearings that took place at Faversham Town Hall on the same day, a large number of prisoners were discharged, including the unfortunate Mrs Burford, who had been arrested as she fled the scene after begging her husband to leave.

On 3 June Nicholas Mears was buried in Boughton-under-Blean churchyard. Two days later Sir William Courtenay and his dead followers were buried in the little churchyard at Hernhill. Before he was buried, Sir William's coffin lid was unscrewed, so that those present, who included a journalist from *The Times*, could view the face of the corpse and be certain that it was indeed Sir William's body. Given the man's ability to convince his followers that he was the risen Christ, it was a wise precaution. Though five days of decay in the June heat had made its mark, and the face was green and sunken, it was still recognisable as the face of the erstwhile Knight of Malta. The coffin was carried through the gate on the north side of the churchyard, and buried to the left of the pathway. The place was deliberately left unmarked. When his death was registered it was under the name of John Tom.

Nicholas Mears' widow was granted a small pension, and Lt Bennett's father received an increase in his pension, but George Catt's widowed mother received a total of only £10 compensation. Eight of John Tom's followers were dead, and sixteen others in gaol, and this brought considerable distress to their dependants, since the authorities were unwilling to grant poor relief to the families of men who were guilty of murder.

A number of people suffered considerable criticism for their role in the affair, notably Lord John Russell and Sir Hussey Vivian for their part in the release of a dangerous lunatic from an asylum. The Church, too, was savaged. 'When religion becomes a trade,' wrote the editor of the *Maidstone Gazette and Kentish Chronicle*, 'and its teachers money-changers, it will astonish nobody that those who have been systematically trained to be duped by methodical knaves, should be occasionally duped by a methodical madman!'

At the Maidstone Assizes in August, Sir William's followers were found guilty of murder. Thomas Mears and William Wills were transported for life and William Price for ten years. All three were sent to Australia. The rest were imprisoned for one year with hard labour, with a month to be spent in solitary confinement.

*The Red Lion at which the bodies lay. (Author's collection)*

*View of the interior of the stable at the Red Lion with six of the bodies. (Author's collection)*

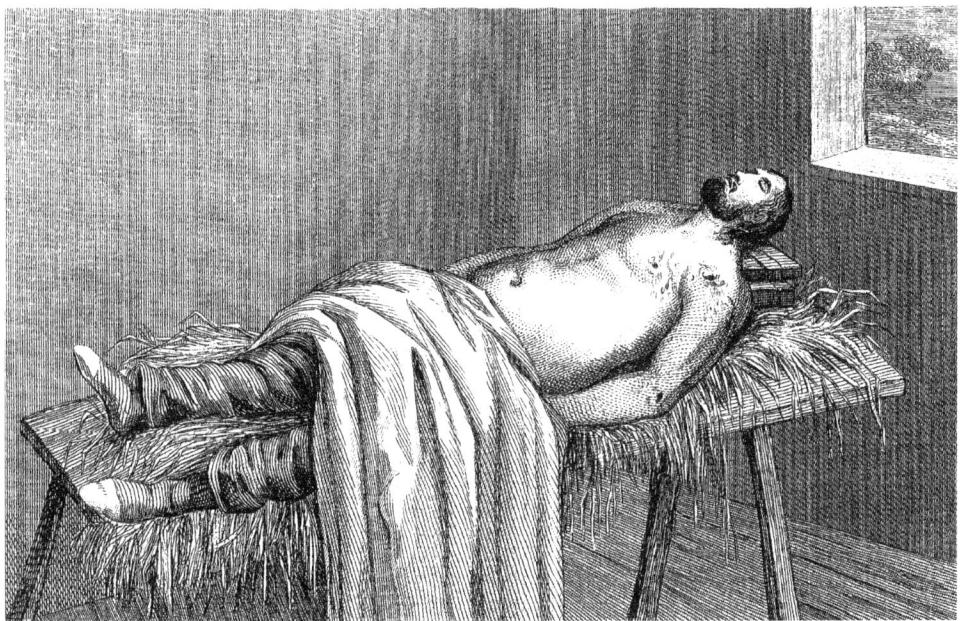
*Sir William Courtenay as he appeared after the post-mortem examination. (Author's collection)*

Some good did eventually emerge from the bloody events of May 1838. The ease with which the people had been duped was used as an argument to improve standards of education. In June 1839 the Government agreed to a substantial increase in its educational grant. In the following month Lord John Russell proposed measures to establish county police constabularies. He made no mention of the Courtenay affair, but he did not need to.

# 4

# THE BODY ON THE BEACH

## *Ramsgate, 1859*

No coastal town can be a stranger to dramatic incident, but in April 1859 an event occurred which was to send the popular seaside resort of Ramsgate into a frenzy of gossip and wild speculation. At 5.45 a.m. on Monday 11 April, forty-seven-year-old Eugene Callahan, a coastguardsman at the Ramsgate station, was near Dumpton Stairs, a flight of steps leading down to the beach below the East Cliff. *The Handbook and Companion to Ramsgate*, published that year, referred to the location as 'a retired spot, much frequented by those who revel in a plunge in the briny sea, without the use of a bathing machine.'

Callahan was patrolling at the top of the cliff near East Cliff Lodge, a Gothic mansion built in 1803 and home of Sir Moses Montefiore, financier and philanthropist, who was currently away in Rome. A man's hat was lying on the beach, and Callahan spotted it and started down to investigate. Some way off he saw Thomas Wilkinson, a thirty-four-year-old boatman, who had been walking close to the cliff picking up shells but was now moving towards what looked to Callahan like the body of a man. He hurried down the stairs and the two men met by the body. The deceased, aged about thirty-five, was naked, and lying on his back, the ebbing tide washing over him. Callahan had naturally assumed that this was a case of drowning, but he now saw that his first impressions had been wrong. The man's left hand had been hacked off at the wrist, and there was a single stab wound on the left side of the chest. There was no sign of a weapon, or of the missing hand, although some clothes lay about 10 yards away. The two men moved the body up the beach close to the cliff, and recovered the clothes, which consisted of a coat, waistcoat, trousers, and a flannel undershirt, but no top shirt. The pockets of the garments were empty and had been turned inside out as if they had been rifled.

*East Cliff Lodge, Ramsgate. (Author's collection)*

*Ramsgate Harbour in 1862. (Author's collection)*

The police were notified, and the Inspector of the Harbour Police ordered that the body should be removed to the pier storeroom. Meanwhile, the beach was being searched for further clues, which were gradually uncovered as the tide ebbed. On some rocks, about 70 or 80 yards from where the body lay, the deceased's boots and umbrella were discovered, together with a hatchet, a linen shirt, a pair of drawers, a neckerchief and a sock. The handle of the hatchet had been sawn short and there were stains on the blade which looked like blood. The wristbands of the shirt had been torn off and the button forcibly ripped from the neck. The missing hand was also found there, with parts of some of the fingers cut from it.

A number of people came to look at the body, either out of curiosity or in the hope that the man could be identified. One man, after observing the injuries, was heard to ask if the deceased had recently been seen in the company of a butcher.

A surgeon was sent for to examine the body. He was forty-three-year-old Henry Curling, member of the Royal College of Surgeons, Licentiate of the Apothecaries Society and general practitioner, who lived at 89 High Street. He arrived at the storeroom just after 8 a.m. and, after an initial assessment, concluded that death had occurred some twelve to fourteen hours previously. He made a more detailed examination later that day together with the assistance of another surgeon, Mr Webster, who also lived and practised in Ramsgate. The main external markings were some rubs on the skin of the forehead and face, which it was thought were caused by the body being washed against rocks by the tide. The eyes were open and the pupils contracted. Directly under the left nipple was a wound, about $1^{1}/_{8}$ inches in length.

*Police sergeant, nineteenth century. (Courtesy of Kent Police Museum)*

The left hand had been detached from the arm by a cut made through the bones of the wrist. Four of the fingers had been cut from the hand, and the thumb was attached by only half an inch of skin at the back. When the fingers were placed in position it showed that three cuts had been made in all, one of which, across the palm had not quite gone all the way through. Examination of the severed digits showed that the middle and forefinger showed scars of previous partial amputations.

The chest wound, which must have been made by a sharp knife, had penetrated the left lung and the left ventricle of the heart. The wound to the heart was some 3 inches in length, which showed that the knife had been moved after it entered the body. Death would have ensued almost immediately. Any external blood had been washed away by the sea, but a considerable quantity was found in the chest cavity. The stomach was full of food with a distinct smell of spirits.

On the following day, the inquest opened at the Town Hall before the coroner, Mr R.J. Emmerson and a jury chaired by Mr W. Stroud. The court was packed with observers. 'The event,' said *The Kentish Gazette*, 'has caused the greatest excitement in the neighbourhood', and indeed Ramsgate was in a ferment of debate about the identity of the victim and how he had met his death, some believing it was the frenzied suicide of a lunatic, others convinced that a brutal murderer was in their midst.

Eugene Callahan described finding the body and said that it could not have arrived in the position where it lay by falling from the cliff. It might, he thought, have got there by the action of the sea.

*East Cliff sands, Ramsgate. (Author's collection)*

Stephen Kingsford, a mariner (it is not clear whether this was Stephen Kingsford senior, aged fifty-nine, or his son of the same name, aged thirty-one, as both were Ramsgate boatmen), had examined the garments of the deceased and seen that there was no cut on the clothing which corresponded to the wound on the chest. He was sure that the body could not have been washed to where it was found, or fallen from the cliff, but speculated that it might have been placed there from a boat.

The immediate question was the man's identity since he was not a resident of Ramsgate. Enquiries had revealed that he had come to stay at The Royal Oak Hotel (then at nos 60 to 64 Harbour Parade; today's Oak Hotel is at no. 66) on the previous Saturday. He had arrived a little after 1 p.m. carrying a carpet-bag in his right hand and an umbrella in his left. He wore a watch and chain, and a gold signet ring on the forefinger of his right hand. There was a dark green stone in the ring with three letters engraved on it. That night, he dined at the hotel with a man called Dane, and breakfasted with the same man the following morning. Whether they knew each other or chanced to share the same table was never established. He had gone to bed at about nine. On the Sunday morning, George Challis, the porter, had seen the man in the passage, studying a railway timetable. Challis had cleaned the man's boots that morning and was rewarded with a shilling. It was apparent that the visitor was a foreigner and spoke very poor English. At about ten o' clock that morning the man left the hotel alone. When he paid his bill, James Medhurst, the waiter, noticed that there were at least ten sovereigns in his 'portemonnaie' as well as some silver.

*Harbour Parade, Ramsgate. (Author's collection)*

The deceased's carpet-bag, umbrella and boots were produced in court, and Challis identified them but added that since he had cleaned them, the boots had been cut shorter in the leg.

It had been possible to trace some of the man's activities in Ramsgate that Sunday. He must have made enquiries about the availability of entertainment in the area, for at three that afternoon he arrived at a house in Falcon Place, the home of fifty-six-year-old Matilda Gibbs, a blacksmith's wife, whose son, Samuel, a twenty-eight-year-old labourer, gave evidence at the inquest. The visitor had told Samuel that he wanted a young woman. Samuel evidently understood exactly what was required and where to go, since he accompanied the man to no. 3 Church Alley, the home of bricklayer's labourer John Brasier. Brasier was a married man with a growing family, but the 1851 census shows that his home was shared with two female lodgers who described their profession as 'needlewoman' and 'dressmaker'. According to Samuel, it was here that the visitor was introduced to a young woman called either Charlotte Nines, Nynes, Nind or Ninds according to the newspapers, and went upstairs with her. When he came downstairs again the man boasted that he had plenty of money and showed Samuel some £40 or £50.

At about seven o' clock that evening, according to John Bugden, landlord of the Crown Inn, Broadstairs, over a mile from the East Cliff, the man entered the inn alone. He carried only an umbrella, and asked for a bottle of bitter ale. He drank alone, did not speak to any other customers, and left twenty minutes later. There was another reported sighting of the same man at about 7.15 p.m., which suggests that one of the witnesses was mistaken either as to the time or the identity of the subject. Mary Jane Lucas, the fifteen-year-old daughter of a widow of Salem Place, Ramsgate, had seen the deceased not far from the spot where his body was found the following morning; 'by the side of Sir Moses Montefiore's wall' walking towards the edge of the cliff. He was alone. Two women and a man were walking in front of her at the time, all going in the opposite direction to the deceased. He was carrying an umbrella but no carpet-bag.

Dr Curling described his examination of the body, saying that it was not possible for him to say whether the hand had been taken off before or after death. He thought the hatchet, produced in evidence, could have detached the hand and fingers but the stab in the chest was made by a sharp knife. The court had to consider the unlikely possibility that the deceased had chopped off his own hand and then stabbed himself, and Curling agreed that this was technically possible. The coroner advised the jury that further enquiries were needed, and the hearing was adjourned for a week.

'A mysterious and brutal murder has been committed in this district, and has occasioned the utmost excitement among the inhabitants,' reported *The Times*, adding, 'The whole affair is involved in inexplicable mystery, which the efforts of the police have proved ineffectual in unravelling.'

This was an unfair comment as the police were making considerable efforts to solve the mystery and as the days passed more information emerged, which was leading them to the conclusion that it was a remarkable case of suicide. The stranger had arrived from America at the end of March, landing at Southampton, and had stayed at the Hotel de L'Europe where he gave a name which sounded like 'Mattinger'. He departed for London on 31 March, where he stayed at Hahn's Hotel, America Square. His left hand was bandaged, which he said was due to an injury he had suffered while on board ship. He declared himself to be a German, travelling for pleasure, and intending to take a tour of Scotland before returning to Germany via Paris. His behaviour during his stay had been entirely rational, although on one occasion, asked to write an address card, he had commented that he had better do it at once as his memory had been very bad since suffering from brain fever while in America.

On Thursday 7 April he travelled by train to Dover, sharing a carriage with a Mr Samuel Kydd. The visitor praised England and the English, and the two men discussed, amongst other things, the price of boots in England and Germany. 'Mattinger' drew attention to the boots he was wearing, which covered the knees, saying that he had had them cut down in length. Kydd noticed that his companion had a bandage on the fingers of his left hand.

On Friday the man travelled from Dover to Deal by omnibus. He was the only passenger, and during the journey a German Bible was either thrown or dropped from the vehicle. It was picked up by a travelling hawker who sold it at the nearby Swingate Inn. The Bible was later examined by the police but had no identifying marks. It was speculated that the visitor had disposed of it to conceal his origins, for from that time onwards in any conversation about his nationality he had declared himself to be Russian. At Deal he went to the Walmer Castle Inn and stayed there one night before travelling to Ramsgate by train.

While at the Royal Oak a gentleman had addressed him in both French and German but the visitor shook his head, saying, 'Me Russ, me Russ'. A void in his Sunday timetable was filled by the new revelation that at half past five that day he visited Miss Catt's oyster shop, where he ate sardines and bread and butter, and drank ale.

*The Times*, reviewing the facts on 18 April, had already made its decision. A reporter had examined the location, accompanied by a local boatman, and had concluded that the deceased had hacked off his own hand, and then stabbed himself. The fingers showed clear signs of earlier healed injuries by which he must have felt he would be identified. 'No circumstance that has happened for many years has created so deep a sensation in East Kent as this shocking affair,' he concluded.

The whole town had undoubtedly been eagerly discussing the mystery and when the inquest re-opened on 20 April the court was, if anything, even more crowded than at the first sitting. There were several new witnesses.

Thomas Green was a cutler of no. 30 York Street, Dover. He had seen the body and identified it as that of a man who had come into his shop at 3 p.m. on Friday 8 April. The man was dressed in a brown shooting coat, brown trousers, and a large hat with a broad brim. Shown the clothes of the deceased he identified them as the same ones. The man had purchased a hatchet and asked Green to cut the handle short so he could more easily pack it in his box. The man was clearly a foreigner and said with a smile that he wanted the hatchet to take home to his own country. Green brought the sawn-off section of the handle, which fitted that of the weapon found.

William Danton Sandwell was a hairdresser of no. 81 King Street, Ramsgate, who said that the visitor had come to his shop at about a quarter past twelve on the Saturday, probably the last thing he did before checking into the Royal Oak. The man, who spoke in broken English, then had a moustache and beard of several months' growth, and asked Sandwell to cut his hair and also shave him, for which he paid 2s.

William Jordan was a waiter at the Elephant and Castle (later the Elephant Hotel) on Margate High Street. At about twenty minutes past eleven on Sunday 10 April the deceased had come into the hotel. He had stayed there for about an hour and during that time had consumed a plate of ham and eggs and two and half pints of ale. He had then gone out leaving his carpet-bag to be looked after, which Jordan said weighed about 25lb, principally from something heavy at the bottom of it. At a quarter past two the man returned, and asked for a drink made from two lemons with cold water. His total bill came to 2s 6d and Jordan received a tip of 2s. He saw the man had silver in his pocket but nothing else. The visitor then took the carpet-bag under his left arm, shook hands with the waiter twice, and left, going in the direction of the railway. He didn't notice anything unusual about the man's left hand.

Shortly afterwards the visitor, carrying his carpet-bag and umbrella, was seen at Margate railway station by John Johns, a boatman of the nearby Margate Coastguard Station, enquiring about the time of the next train to Ramsgate. The train wasn't due until 4.35 p.m. so the stranger wandered in the direction of Royal Crescent. Some time later Johns saw him return without the bag. Mr Aldridge, the chief coastguard officer, also saw the man and asked him if he had come off a ship. The man seemed annoyed by this question and exclaimed, 'No, no ship!' in a very excited manner. The following morning Johns had found the carpet-bag in the water not far from Royal Crescent. It was empty. He was sure that it could not have been washed there by the sea but must have been placed there.

William Riddell, who lived opposite the Six Bells pub in Margate, said that on the Monday morning he had been passing by Royal Crescent wall and found two linen shirts, two collars, a white pocket handkerchief and a clothes brush. One shirt had been found stuffed between the stones of a wall, and the other had been covered lightly with sand. They were dry and had been tied up with worsted. All were produced in evidence. The shirts resembled the one found at Ramsgate and all had had their identifying marks picked out.

At this point the observers in court must have prepared themselves for a sensation for the next witness was Charlotte, the woman with whom the stranger had passed some time at Mr Brasier's. Charlotte revealed that she was married but separated from her husband and was living with her mother at no. 3 Church Street, just round the corner from Brasier's house. She confirmed that the stranger had been brought to her by Samuel Gibbs, and after some conversation, presumably of a business nature, she took him round the corner to Brasier's and went upstairs with him. Her customer's left hand was wrapped in a bandage and he smelt of liquor. The pair remained together for a quarter of an hour. She noticed that he wore a watch and chain which appeared to be made of gold. Business done, he gave her 3s 6d. Gibbs had been downstairs waiting for him and asked him for money to buy drink. At first the man said he had no small change but eventually found sixpence in his pocket and handed Gibbs his commission.

The last people to see the deceased alive were Charlotte Maxted, a servant, and her sweetheart George Jackson. They were walking on the East Parade at 8 p.m. on Sunday evening. It was a bright moonlit night. The man was walking slowly, arms folded and his hat over his eyes, in the direction of Augusta Stairs, a flight of stone steps leading down from the East Cliff Promenade to the sands. It was probably this same couple who later saw the stranger sitting alone on some rocks at the water's edge between half past eight and nine o' clock.

For some reason Riddell was recalled. Perhaps he had indicated that he had something more to say, for he now revealed that near the clothes previously described he had found the upper part of a shirt stained with blood. There were no holes in it, but the armholes had been cut away. He left it where he had found it. Something in Riddell's attitude must have excited suspicion, since the coroner expressed his opinion that, 'from the manner in which this witness gave his evidence, that little reliance could be placed upon it.'

Superintendent James Livick of the Ramsgate police then produced a scrap of paper which had been found near the body in the storehouse, presumably as part of the debris picked up on the beach. It was a letter written in pencil. When found, the paper was wet, folded up, and appeared to have been kept in a pocket. Fortunately a translator was at hand. Maurice Labatt, a seventy-year-old shipping agent's clerk born in Holstein, then living at no. 9 Uppingham Place, testified that the words were in German, the work of an uneducated man, badly written and badly spelt. One expression was 'peculiar' and might have been written by a Dutchman. The letter read:

Dear mother, – Here are five dollars, – little, but from a good heart.
Henry Matterigh. [sic]

There was no way of determining if the carrier of the letter was also the man who had written it.

While the jury was digesting this information, Superintendent Prichard of the Royal Harbour Police produced in evidence the clothing of the deceased, together with a solid piece of chalk which had been cut from a rock about 500ft nearer the sea from where the body had been found. On it were four distinct marks. The hatchet was brought and its blade was shown to fit the marks exactly. Both the

*The steps leading down to the beach at Dumpton, Ramsgate, 2008. (Author's collection)*

hatchet and the pieces of the hand and fingers had been found a few yards from the rock.

Dr Curling was recalled. He may have examined the body again, and now stated that from the retraction of the tendons in the fingers, he had concluded that the injuries to the hand had happened while the deceased was alive, but believed they could not have been defensive wounds. If the blows had been given by a third party that person 'must have stood in the same position towards the hands as the deceased himself.'

A boatman called Solley said he believed that had the body fallen near the rocks it could have been swept by the tide to the position some eighty or ninety yards away where it was eventually found, but when Eugene Callahan was recalled, he said that he did not think this was possible.

The jury considered its verdict in the face of this conflicting and confusing evidence. Eventually they found that, 'The deceased died from a wound in the left breast, between the evening of the 10th and morning of the 11th, but by whom inflicted there is not sufficient evidence to show.'

There the matter was allowed to rest, but the public was far from satisfied. The identity of the man was still unclear (the name under which he checked into the hotel was never revealed). True, he had been behaving a little oddly, but in 1859 the mere fact that he was a foreigner was quite sufficient to explain that. It was possible that there was a logical explanation for his behaviour which further knowledge of his identity and background would reveal. If he had been murdered, then a brutal killer was on the loose, and many people, anxious that the police were ignoring public safety to put the case down as one of suicide, wrote to the press demanding action. After all, if he had stabbed himself, where was the knife? And the fact that his money, watch and ring were missing naturally suggested that he had been robbed.

The *Kentish Observer* stated that:

It is an enigma from beginning to end, wrapped in darkness dense and terrible as the darkness of the grave in which the stranger now reposes. Unknown – unclaimed – no stone preserves the memory of his name; no tablet deplores the sadness of his fate; but he will long dwell in the recollection of the townspeople, who will not cease to speculate on the cause of his death, and to hope that something may one day turn up to dispel the impenetrable mystery in which it is involved.

On 7 May a long letter was published in *The Times* under the heading 'The Murder at Ramsgate' with a detailed analysis of the case. The author, writing from Ramsgate, signed himself 'C.D.' and, from his observations, must have been present at the inquest. Pointing out that when the boots were produced in evidence, a juryman, who was a shoemaker, had commented that they appeared to have been cut down by someone 'in that trade'; he urged that this was something that ought to have been investigated. C.D. was not as dismissive of Riddell's testimony as the coroner and added what *The Times* omitted to report, that this witness had stated that the bloody shirt was of a similar kind as the clean ones. Riddell had also claimed that he saw marks near the spot, as if a man and woman had knelt down, and also a burnt match and the appearance of something having been burnt there. C.D. saw nothing suspicious in the purchase of the hatchet. 'Such a purchase is by no means an uncommon thing at the seaside, especially with foreigners.' He pointed out that there was no proof at all that the German Bible belonged to the visitor, and implied that even if it did it might simply have been lost rather than deliberately disposed of.

C.D. also thought that the evidence of Samuel Gibbs had been insufficiently sifted at the inquest, the coroner commenting that he considered it to be of little value. The writer referred to Gibbs' statement, that he had seen the deceased with as much as £50, and that the man had also promised to take him for a ride the following morning.

Was C.D. implying that Gibbs, abetted possibly by Charlotte (the lady of ill-repute), had robbed and murdered the victim for his money? Ignoring the evidence of John Johns, who had found the carpet-bag in Margate, C.D. suggested that the man had taken it back with him to Ramsgate, and left it with someone when he went out for a walk. He was surprised that the two surgeons had convinced themselves that the deceased had been able to stab himself, after having inflicted the many wounds on his hand, while faint from pain and loss of blood. Even Dr Curling had said at first that it was not certain that the hand had been detached in life. C.D. smelt possible corruption:

> It is well known that these surgeons were not the only medical gentlemen who saw the body, and who could have given evidence on the subject. Was the evidence of those other gentlemen kept back because their opinion was unfavourable to the view of suicide? Or at all events, was it not easy to procure a surgeon from Dover, Canterbury, or even London?

C.D. dismissed the suicide theory, pointing out that all those who came into contact with the visitor had testified that he appeared to be perfectly sane:

> I do not hesitate to say that the facts to my mind clearly prove that a foul and brutal murder has been committed ... that he was murdered in some house at Ramsgate, and as there is every reason to believe, while he was in a recumbent position, seems highly probable.

He added, 'Those who know Ramsgate are well aware that the least reputable part of the town borders on some open ground and fields, over which you can go directly to the cliff, underneath which the body was found.' He believed that on a dark night, anyone who knew the area could avoid being seen by patrolling coastguards. If the body had been let down by a rope it would account for the abrasions, as it rubbed against the cliff.

C.D. urged that the circumstances were such that pressure should be brought to bear for a Government enquiry. 'There is, moreover, a strong and general feeling that much evidence exists in this case which either has not yet been discovered or has been intentionally withheld from the public.'

These were provocative words, and many agreed with the anonymous writer. Two letters were published in *The Times* on 9 May. Samuel Kydd, the travelling companion of 7 April, wrote, 'He was essentially a sane man, judging from appearance and conversation, as unlikely to commit suicide as any man I ever met.' Referring to the cut down boots, he asked that the deceased's boots should be examined, since if they were cut above the knee this proved that it had been done before 7 April.

Frederick Gant, surgeon and 'pathological anatomist' of the Royal Free Hospital, also wrote to *The Times*, pointing out that while the position and direction of the wound was not incompatible with it being self-inflicted, 'All the evidence points in one direction – to a most savage murder – and the whole matter ought to be raked up and pursued to the very bottom.'

John Mortlock Daniell, described by the *Kentish Observer* as 'a dissenting minister of some notoriety in our town', published a tract on the case in which he argued strongly that it was a case of murder. Daniell pointed out that the stranger was known to mix with bad company and had probably lost his fingers in an earlier skirmish, suggesting that he had bought the hatchet as a weapon of self defence. He believed that the man had gone down to the beach to bathe, and after he undressed, robbers went to the garments to plunder them. The victim was murdered defending his property, and the killers had then chopped off the hand so he could not be identified.

Despite the inconclusive result of the inquest, the police had been continuing their efforts to discover the dead man's identity. Having established that the visitor had arrived in Southampton on the *Bremen* from New York, Superintendent Livick had written to the New York police, giving them all the known facts of the case. On 28 May he received a reply. The deceased was a German called Frederick (or Friedrich) Mattern. He had arrived in New York from Germany about two years previously, and

*East Cliff and beach, Ramsgate, 2008. (Author's collection)*

was known to be 'a person of reserved manners, but not hypochondriacal nor subject to aberration of mind.' He had two brothers, Henry and Jacob, also living in New York, and they were not in good circumstances. Their parents, Jacob and Catherine, lived at 'Wolfstein Rheinfels, Bayer, Germany.' Mattern was a butcher by profession. About fourteen months ago, he had been using a machine to cut meat for sausages, when he had accidentally severed the joints of the second and forefinger of his left hand. He had sailed on the *Bremen* on 19 March with the intention of returning to Germany. He then had with him the sum of between $160 and $250. The message he carried had been written not by himself but his brother, and presumably he had intended to pass on the letter and a gift of $5 to his mother on his return to Germany. *The Times* reporter recalled the man who, on seeing the wounds, had asked if the deceased had been seen with a butcher. It was speculated that Mattern had somehow lost all his money, and determined to commit suicide, first taking care to do everything he could to conceal his identity, including removing the hand with its distinctive injuries, presumably to spare his family. His missing property could, it was conjectured, have been stolen after death.

Officially, the case remains unsolved.

# 5

# THE MAN WHO WANTED TO BE HANGED

## *Chatham, 1862*

Chatham's importance in British Naval history began in 1568 when Queen Elizabeth I established a naval dockyard, and the town expanded to serve the new industry. Many hundreds of ships were launched at Chatham, and HMS *Victory* was built there. A line of earthworks was constructed to protect the vital dockyards, officially called the Great Lines of Defence, but known locally as the 'Chatham Lines'. In the event, the dockyard never came under the expected attack, but the stout defences can still be seen today.

In 1858 the East Kent line brought the railway to Chatham and in the following year this became a part of the London, Chatham and Dover railway. The tracks ran underneath the Chatham Lines, and in places, air vents had to be constructed. This left an uneven heaping of chalk and bricks on the surface covering some two acres of land and about 20ft high at its highest point. The chalk piles were a playground for local boys and ideal for a game of 'hunt the hare' – what we would now call 'hide and seek'.

The Houghton family was one of many who were closely connected with the town's naval industry. They lived in Alma Place, Chatham, just off the High Street. William, who was born about 1794, had been a gunner in the Royal Navy, although by 1851 he had retired on a pension. His wife Lucy, some twenty years his junior, kept a small grocery shop. The couple had married in 1835 and had five sons. In 1861 two of the Houghton boys, William and Aaron, were serving in the Royal Navy and George worked as a barge-boy in the Chatham Dockyards. Twelve-year-old John, who had been born at sea, would also join the Navy. Their youngest boy, presumably destined for a similar career, was Thomas Frederick Houghton, born in 1852. A cheerful lad, always in a good humour, he was well known for going about singing happily to himself.

*Chatham and Rochester from the Lines, Gillingham. (Author's collection)*

Early on the afternoon of Wednesday 23 July 1862 Thomas left his home to play on Chatham Lines. Each evening the area was crowded with men and boys playing cricket and other games, but it was 2 p.m., and few people were about. His absence for a number of hours does not appear to have excited any concern.

Shortly after five o' clock, thirteen-year-old Albert Tree, who lived at Park Place, Brompton, left school and hurried up to the Lines with seven other boys where, in a wheatfield belonging to a Mr Gilbert, they played at 'hunt the hare'. The boys had been at play for over half an hour when, running around a chalk-heap to hide from his playmates, Albert saw the body of a dead boy and a great deal of blood on the ground. At that moment he saw two men coming up the path towards him, one of whom was Chatham bricklayer Thomas Everist, and he at once ran to tell them what he had seen. Everist, who recognised the dead child as Thomas Houghton, felt the body and found the boy quite dead and cold. He at once sent Albert to tell the police, and remained with the body until Police Sergeant Fisher came. The child was lying on his back with both arms raised. Fisher saw that the boy's throat had been cut and there was a great deal of blood on the face, neck and shirt, and blood on the grass near the head. He also saw a pool of blood some 6 or 7ft away and a spot of blood near the pathway. The boy's clothes were disturbed, although there was no sign that any sexual violence had taken place. Marks found on the ground nearby suggested that the child had given up his life only after a tremendous struggle.

A surgeon, Mr George William Locke, was sent for, and he hurried to the spot to view the body in place. George Houghton was returning from work when he learned of his brother's murder, and at once went to the chalk heap where he saw the body.

*Chatham Dockyard. (Author's collection)*

Fisher then directed that the body should be moved to the Napier Arms Tavern, Brompton. The news of the tragic find spread rapidly around the area, and that same day, the spot where the body was found was visited by a large number of people.

On the following day a post-mortem examination took place, the police taking possession of the clothing. Locke found a deep stab wound in the boy's throat, which had penetrated the larynx, and was sufficient to cause death from asphyxia. The face was bruised as if from a heavy blow on the right cheek and there were bruises on the back and both thighs. There were marks of compression on the throat which he thought had been caused by the tie.

The district coroner, Mr T. Hills, at once empanelled a jury and after taking formal evidence of the identity of the deceased and the finding of the body, adjourned for a week to enable the police to make their enquiries.

Between eleven and midnight the following evening, Police Constable Stephen Hibbert no. 469 was on duty in the stables of Superintendent Everist of the County Police. Robert Alexander Burton, a youth of eighteen, his clothing very dirty, and his shirtsleeves rolled up, entered the stable and said, 'Do you want a job to take me to the station-house?' He then gave himself up for the murder of Thomas Houghton. Hibbert immediately took him to the home of Superintendent Everist, who lived only four doors away from the Houghtons in Alma Place. On the way, Burton showed some anxiety, saying, 'You are not going to take me to the boy's mother, are you?' Hibbert said he was not. Arriving at Everist's house Hibbert called the superintendent downstairs.

While they waited, Burton, impatient to tell his story, launched into a confession. He said he had stabbed Thomas in the neck with a knife, and when he was down,

*Chatham harbour, 1829. (Author's collection)*

trod on his face and neck, then knelt on the belly and pressed his hands on the throat until the blood gushed from the boy's nose and mouth. Everist hurried downstairs only partly dressed, to be told of Burton's confession to the murder of the child, whom he had known for five years. After the usual caution, Burton made a full statement. He said he was tired of life and wanted to be hanged, so he had determined to kill someone, and didn't care who that might be. He had been walking along the street and chancing to see the boy and his mother, decided that the child would be his victim. He followed them, and saw the mother enter her house after giving the child permission to play on the Lines. It was then about 2 p.m., and he followed the boy to the spot near the chalk outcrops. Accosting the unsuspecting child he knocked him down and dragged him a short way to where he could carry out the crime unobserved. The boy struggled valiantly and tried to get free, but Burton was able to get his knife from his pocket and make a deep cut across the throat, severing the windpipe. Even after receiving this terrible wound the boy continued to fight back, and seized his attacker's hands, but Burton shook him off, and finding that the victim did not 'die quick enough' he knelt on the child and squeezed his throat until he was dead. The superintendent commented on the bruises on the boy's face but Burton denied being responsible for those. He said that after the crime his hands were covered in blood and he had wiped them as best he could on the boy's shirt.

Burton said that after committing the murder he had hurried across the Lines. A gentleman dressed in black was coming towards him, and realising that his hands were still bloody, Burton had thrust them into the pockets of his trousers. He then

*A police constable in the nineteenth century. (Courtesy of Kent Police Museum)*

went to the military bathing pond where he washed his hands, face and clothes, and cleaned the blood from the knife. Later he walked into the town, and that night hid the knife in the water-closet of the Dark Sun public house on Chatham High Street.

Everist, who had known Burton for four years and was aware of him as an unstable character, may well have been in some doubt as to whether this was a genuine confession or the result of a delusion. Burton, sensing that doubt, rolled down his shirtsleeves and showed Everist that they were bloodstained from where the boy had caught hold of his arms. On searching the prisoner, further bloodstains were found on his scarf, trouser legs, and inside the trouser pockets. The police at once went with Burton to the Dark Sun where the knife, a common dinner knife ground down to a sharp point, was found where the prisoner had said it was. Further enquiries revealed that the knife had been given to Burton by George Deacon, a local cooper, but it had not then been ground down to a point. They later examined the victim's shirt and saw in the bloodstains the marks of the hands that had been wiped on the fabric.

The Burton family lived only a few hundred yards from the Houghtons at the back of no. 185 High Street. Robert's father, Thomas, had been a convict guard but after being pensioned from that service became a labourer in the Chatham Dockyards, and by 1862 he was a 'leading man of labourers'. Robert was their eighth child, born in 1844. He was known to have been a difficult child and certainly became a wayward teenager, violent and bad tempered, occasionally prone to bouts of strange behaviour, unable to settle on a career or stick to any occupation. He had a history of committing serious assaults on people who had given him offence. His father had done his best to find him a suitable career, apprenticing him to a builder in Rochester called Andrews, but Burton had not worked there long before he suddenly went missing for several days. On his return, looking weak and footsore, he told Andrews that he had been to Canterbury to enlist as a soldier, but while in the barracks he had changed his mind and run all the way home. He settled back into his work for a while but then went missing a second time. On his return Andrews kindly decided to give him another chance, hoping that he would mend his behaviour, but at the end of 1860, Burton deserted his master for the third time, taking with him his tools, which he later pawned. He went to Portsmouth where he tried to get taken onto one of Her Majesty's ships, but when enquiries were made about him, it was discovered that he was a bound apprentice which prevented his being accepted. While there he ate dinner at a tavern, and being asked to pay the sum of 2s 6d and being short of money he struck the waiter in the chest knocking him down, threw a pickle jar at him, and ran. He returned to Chatham, where even the patient Mr Andrews washed his hands of the youth, and Burton's father, too, would have nothing more to do with him.

Burton joined the West Kent Militia in Maidstone, but deserted with his bounty money, part of which he spent in a brothel, the rest being stolen from him. He then went to work for a shoemaker called William Clarke on Chatham High Street, and was living with him in 1861, although his occupation in that census is described as carpenter. He was sent out one day on an errand, but absconded with money he had received for his master. In January 1862 he was taken before the Rochester magistrates on a charge of theft. Sentenced to two months with hard labour, he told the magistrates he would revenge himself on Clarke when he was released. Clarke may well have taken this threat seriously because by the time Burton was free he had left Chatham. At the time of the murder, Burton's most recent occupations had been occasional work as a porter or as a waiter in public houses.

On Friday 25 July, Burton was brought before the county magistrates at the justice room, Rochester, where he was charged with the wilful murder of Thomas Frederick Houghton. Burton was just eighteen, rather short for his age, and might have been taken for younger. He treated the proceedings with an air of indifference. Lucy Houghton, the boy's mother, made a pitiful sight in court, and was so affected by distress that she could barely be heard. Before she gave evidence the magistrates ordered that the knife be removed from the exhibits table so she would not see it. When Burton was asked if he had any reason to offer why he should not be remanded until Monday, he replied boldly that he would rather be tried that day if he could. As he was conducted to the van to take him to the cells Burton was assailed by cries of execration from a mob, mainly composed of women, who had assembled outside the court, and he was heard to say that he would like to serve the women the same way as he had treated the boy. He added that since the case against him was so clear, the magistrates could have proceeded with his examination at once without remanding him.

*Chatham High Street, 1904. (Author's collection)*

At his request, Everist took Burton to the Lines and the prisoner pointed out the place where the crime had been committed. Here, in a rare moment of remorse, Burton confided to the policeman that he did not want to see the boy's mother as this was the only thing that touched him. He added that it was a fortunate thing for his late employer, Mr Clarke, that he had left the town, as he was the man he had really wanted to kill.

On 29 July Burton was brought up before a bench of magistrates at Rochester by Superintendent Everist. Large crowds assembled in the streets of Chatham and Rochester to see him as he was driven to the court. Burton listened attentively to the evidence, occasionally correcting the witnesses – he said he had never touched the boy's tie but had strangled him with his hands. It was reported that, 'During the whole of the examination the prisoner displayed the greatest possible levity.' He was committed for trial and removed from the dock 'apparently unconcerned'.

The counsel appointed to Burton was William Ribton, a Sligo-born barrister adept at employing every available means to engage the sympathies of the jury for his clients. He recognised at once that the only possible defence in Burton's case was insanity. It is not clear why Ribton did not invoke 'The Trial of Offences Act 1856' (often called the Palmer Act after William Palmer of Rugeley, for whose benefit it was enacted) which would have enabled the trial to take place elsewhere than Maidstone, as it would not have been hard to prove that local feeling would prevent the possibility of a fair trial. Ribton concentrated instead on assembling his defence of insanity, knowing that the delay that would ensue would allow public outrage

*Maidstone Gaol, 1829. (Author's collection)*

*Exterior of Maidstone Gaol. (Author's collection)*

to cool. Thus in December 1862 the case came before the Maidstone Assizes, with Ribton asking for more time to assemble his evidence and suggesting that his client might be unfit to plead. *The Times* observed dryly:

> When the prisoner was brought to the bar he certainly showed no symptoms of insanity, unless it was an apparent unconcern. He is a short, sharp-looking youth, and looked round the crowded court without the least sense of his situation.

Ribton's application was granted, and the trial finally opened on Wednesday 18 March 1863 at Maidstone Assizes.

There was some difficulty in selecting a jury. Mr Barrow, counsel for the prosecution, objected to any Maidstone men being selected as there was an association in the town which campaigned against capital punishment. Mr Ribton, on the other hand, objected to Chatham or Rochester men. Once men from those towns were excluded, however, it was found that an insufficient number of candidates remained to form a jury. A compromise was finally reached in which only Maidstone and Chatham men were excluded.

Brought to the bar, Burton at once pleaded guilty, upon which Ribton took the opportunity to announce to the court that his client suffered from the delusion that he wanted to hang, but Mr Justice Wightman, seeing what Ribton was up to, interrupted, 'with great firmness of voice and tone' and advised that a plea of not guilty did not mean that the prisoner denied responsibility, but was no more than a statement that he wished to be put on trial, and it was far better for all purposes that he do so. Burton, listening to the judge's warning words, 'with apparent intelligence', at once acceded to them. The jurors, who had just been asked to believe that the prisoner laboured under an insane delusion, took due note of this reaction.

Mr Barrow in his opening address reminded the jury that every man was presumed sane until the contrary was proved. He saw no evidence of insanity, the prisoner having given a clear and sensible account of the crime, and of the feelings under which he had committed it. The prosecution witnesses were brought and Burton listened to them with great attention. Mr Ribton did not dispute the facts, but put forward his defence of insanity relying on two previous cases, James Hadfield, who had fired a pistol at George III in 1800 and was acquitted on the grounds of insanity, and the better known Daniel M'Naghten, tried for murder in 1843 and acquitted. M'Naghton believed he was the victim of an international conspiracy and shot Edward Drummond, Robert Peel's secretary, mistaking him for the Prime Minister. As a result of the latter case a panel of judges had been formed which laid down the guidelines for juries regarding insanity. Under the M'Naghten Rules, as they came to be known:

> It must be clearly proved that, at the time of the committing of the act, the party accused was labouring under such a defect of reason, from disease of the mind, as not to know the nature and quality of the act he was doing; or, if he did know it, that he did not know he was doing what was wrong.

Ribton, who must have known that he was stretching things a little, maintained that this did not go far enough if the accused was shown to labour under delusions.

He then brought evidence of a hereditary trait of insanity in the family, something which can only have added to the already acute distress of the Burtons. Robert's mother had twice been admitted to a lunatic asylum, and though now at home 'was under some degree of aberration'. A brother was 'nearly lunatic' and the prisoner had always been eccentric and strange in his behaviour, and there were 'proofs of a depraved and perverted mind.' He had 'been known to kill cats and put them in a pie and send them to the bakehouse.' (At this, Burton smiled.) Ribton then proposed the theory of 'homicidal mania' and here he read from the classic authority, *Taylor on Medical Jurisprudence*, which states that a person suffering from homicidal mania is unable to avoid the impulse to murder. It was, he said, 'insanity of the moral feelings.'

The witnesses for the defence were then brought. Mr Andrews, to whom Burton had been apprenticed in 1859, said that the boy had a 'very vacant look' and 'when told to do anything would often run about, looking up to the sky as if he were a maniac.' He had run away in May 1860 and came back 'in a most wretched state', saying he had been to Canterbury to try and enlist as a soldier and had been in the barracks and had run back the whole way. He stayed a few months and then went away again. Andrews took him back on his return but in the early part of 1861 Burton went to Portsmouth and came back after ten days. Andrews had had enough. He would not take his apprentice back and with the father's consent, burnt the indentures.

Other witnesses were brought to say that they had observed Burton's vacancy of mind, and sudden changes of mood, and that the prisoner had been seen to eat soap and bite a candle. Mr Ribton then suffered an unpleasant surprise. He brought a witness to prove the story that Burton had baked a cat in a pie, but it emerged that the idea of killing the cat had been that of another boy. Once it was killed, the prisoner had said he would eat a piece of it, and cut a piece off the hindquarters and ate it. The cat had indeed been sent to the bakehouse but asked by whom, the witness said, 'we all put it in a pie and sent it.' The whole story now seemed less like evidence of insanity than of a cruel and senseless group prank, born of idleness.

Mr Fayle, a Chatham surgeon, stated that he had twice sent Robert's mother Ann to an asylum. She had been 'low and desponding' and had attempted suicide. The brother was 'of weak intellect ... peculiar looking and dissipated.' He believed that Burton laboured under 'moral insanity, that is, he knows perfectly well what he is doing, but has no control over himself.' So saying, Dr Fayle sealed the fate of his patient, if it had not already been sealed. Mr Ribton wanted to ask the witness if he considered the prisoner to have been sane or insane at the time of the murder, but an increasingly skeptical Justice Wightman refused to allow the question. That, he said, was the very question the jury was to determine.

That closed the evidence for the defence, but the prosecution now brought witnesses to rebut the suggestion that Burton was insane. Mr Harold, a medical attendant at the county prison, said he had seen no evidence of insanity and was cross-examined by Ribton who asked if he thought if a man with a desire to be hanged was labouring under a delusion. Harold agreed, upon which Wightman pointedly interjected; 'What is the delusion under which you suppose he would be labouring?' a question which the witness, in a state of some perplexity, was unable to answer with any clarity.

Ribton summed up the evidence for the defence, insisting that his client's vehement desire to be hanged was the strongest proof of insanity. Mr Barrow had a simpler task before him. The law, as it then stood, was entirely on his side. If a man knew right from wrong, and that he was committing an offence against the laws of God and nature, he was considered to be sane. Learned counsel, said Barrow, had confounded insanity with depravity. There was no evidence of delusions. The defence had argued that a defect in the moral faculties was tantamount to insanity, but then all criminality must to some degree involve some moral defect. Under this argument, there could be no such thing as criminality, since any crime would secure a perfect impunity. The moral gentleman of the jury must have shuddered at the concept.

Mr Justice Wightman in his summing up made it clear to the jury that the only question in the case was whether the prisoner was responsible for his actions.

In the case of Hadfield, there was evidence of head wounds which had injured his brain. He asked the jury to apply the M'Naghten test, and compare it to the defence plea of 'moral insanity' under which a man killed another on an uncontrollable impulse, while perfectly aware that it was wrong to do so. 'This would appear to be a most dangerous doctrine, and fatal to the interest of society and security of life. Surely such a theory was as contrary to common sense as it undoubtedly was to law?' He added that the fact that the prisoner committed the crime in order to be hanged showed clearly that he was well aware that his action was against the law.

The jurors, though faced with one of the harshest decisions many of them would ever have to make, had had their paths considerably eased. There was no doubt as to the guilt of the prisoner, and by finding him guilty they would not only be acting with common sense, and according to the law, they would be protecting society. It took them fifteen minutes to come back with a verdict of guilty. The verdict, commented *The Times*, 'seemed to give general satisfaction.'

Wightman addressed Burton 'in a very emphatic tone':

> you are guilty of a murder more barbarous and inhuman than any which has come under my cognizance during a judicial experience of upwards of twenty years ... I could not trust myself to dwell upon its shocking details ... For such a crime as yours there can be no hope of mercy in this world.

He then passed sentence of death. Burton listened throughout with serious attention, assuming at the end his habitual air of callous indifference. After a pause of a few moments, in which it seemed that a sense of awe was struggling with his desire to take a tone of bravado, he seemed almost to force himself to brazen it out, and with an impudent smile thanked his lordship and went quickly down from the dock, followed by an audible murmur, and what was very nearly a cry of horror from the densely crowded audience.

Back in gaol, Burton continued breezily unconcerned as to his fate. He asked his gaolers for an additional allowance of food and also some beer, which he said he believed was always given to prisoners under sentence of death, adding that if he was entitled to some tobacco he would like some of that, too. On being told that he was entitled only to the usual prison rations he flew into a rage, threatening that he would 'cause some trouble yet.' Eventually, under the orders of the medical officer, two half pints of porter were allowed to him daily. 'The culprit does not appear to entertain the slightest fear of death,' reported the *Chatham News and North Kent Spectator*, 'on the contrary, he actually seems to exult at the prospect that awaits him.' He was visited by some of his relations but shocked them by his absence of any contrition for his crime, and refused to see the prison chaplain, Charles Edward Shirley Woolmer, saying he would as soon see the Devil.

The trial had had one important effect. It had created considerable public debate on the issue of 'moral insanity', which Dr Higginson Fayle maintained in a letter to the *Chatham News* was very different from moral depravity. 'The murderous impulse was stronger and more uncontrollable than reason, and reason was overthrown by it.' Fayle also revealed that in addition to the insanity on the mother's side of the family, Thomas Burton had a sister in an asylum. 'Public safety demands his close confinement,' said Fayle, 'but public justice requires that his life should be spared.'

In general, however, the press applauded the verdict. *The Saturday Review* commented: 'To Justice Wightman society is under a deep debt of gratitude for the indignant scorn with which he brushed away the medical fallacies on this doctrine of homicidal mania ...'

Society was slow to request Burton's reprieve but eventually a petition was sent to the Home Secretary, Sir George Grey, who responded that there was nothing to warrant his intervention. The execution was scheduled for 18 April. Despite the chaplain's best efforts, Burton remained unrepentant. On the Sunday after his conviction he behaved in a disorderly manner in chapel, and afterwards said he would have nothing more to do with religion, threatening to burn any books that might be given to him on the subject. The Bible, he declared, had said that no man could serve two masters and he was a servant of the Devil.

On 1 April Burton received a visit from his sister and aunt. They passed him a paper with a hymn written on it by his little nephew, George. He behaved towards them with the same bold indifference he had shown before, laughing at their expressions of sorrow, and they returned home shocked and distressed. As the day progressed, however, his courage in the face of imminent death began to ebb away. He read the note from his nephew and was suddenly flooded with emotion. Sobbing bitterly, he sent for the chaplain, and confessed his deep sorrow for his crime, apologising for his past conduct, which he said had been just bravado. From that time onwards he was regularly attended by the chaplain, and earnestly listened to his words, declaring that he wished only to prepare himself for his fate. On the following day he wrote a letter to his sister:

> I thought on the way in which I treated you, and the pain I must have given you to see me so careless and stubborn in my awful position; that when I came to myself it truly grieved me from my heart ...

Having no hope of any mercy and knowing that he was facing the last few days of his short life, he determined to devote his remaining time to seeking forgiveness from the Almighty. He begged his sister to come and see him again and bring George. He also sent his love to his father and begged for a visit or at least a letter to say that he had forgiven 'his disgraceful son'. A few days later Burton received a letter from his father, who stated that he could not come to see him as parting under those circumstances would be too painful, but he readily forgave him his past misconduct. This resulted in a letter of effusive gratitude in which he advised his father and his brother James, 'Do not go any longer in sin and drunkenness ,' saying that, 'Ever since I knew you to be my father you have been serving that hard taskmaster the Devil ...' urging him that it was not too late to repent. Burton's mother, in view of her 'low and desponding condition', was not even aware of the crime her son had committed. All news of it was kept from her, for fear that her mind would be further affected.

Much of Burton's remaining time was taken up in reading scriptures. In his last week he was visited by his brother and two nephews, and told them he had no desire to live but believed his life had been justly forfeited. A day or two before his execution he sent for a friend and showed him the hymns of a deeply penitential nature which had most comforted him.

He made a full confession of all his misdeeds to the chaplain, tracing the start of his downfall to the fact that his first master, a grocer, had left the till unlocked by which he was tempted to steal, and saying he had been misled by bad company. He had initially wanted to kill the landlady of the Little Crown public house he had once frequented, as she had forbidden him to enter the premises again, but he had given up the idea as too difficult. He knew that failure might lead only to transportation, and he wanted to be hanged. To ensure his execution he determined to kill a boy or woman he could easily master. He had always had a longing for death on the scaffold, from a love of notoriety, and also to punish his father, who had turned him out of the house saying he would not walk across the street to save him from the gallows. He had intended to kill the boy first and the landlady afterwards, but the horror of the crime had affected him and he had decided to give himself up.

On 9 April a gentleman from Chatham was with him in his cell for an hour, and was convinced that the religious change was genuine. He found Burton perfectly calm, reposing in the hope of forgiveness through his saviour.

Even after Burton's sudden conversion he hesitated about contacting Mrs Houghton, saying, 'I have thought of it but I was afraid it would bring it all up again and make the poor woman suffer it all over again.' Mrs Houghton had had further trials to bear since she had been recently widowed. Finally Burton agreed to let the chaplain act as intermediary, and on 10 April Woolmer wrote to Lucy Houghton, and asked if she could write down that she forgave Burton, as she herself hoped to be forgiven. Burton also wrote to her, though whether his words comforted her or not is unknown. He told her of her son's last moments, when he had cried 'pray, pray', and then, 'I'm a dying, I'm a dying', then 'he went off very calm to that place where sorrow never entereth.' Burton said he had repented for his 'awful crime' and asked her forgiveness. Lucy replied that her boy's fate had caused great distress in the family and caused the death of his father. She expressed her sympathy for Robert's mother, and 'with a heart full of grief', she forgave him.

As early as three o' clock on the morning of Saturday 18 April, an orderly crowd was seen proceeding towards Maidstone. Asked by the police where they were going at so early an hour the people, who included many women then politely referred to as 'unfortunates', said they were 'going to see a man hanged.' As the day progressed more and more pedestrians hurried along the highways leading from Chatham and Rochester to Maidstone, while carts and cabs conveyed still more eager sightseers, and others travelled by train. Before the hour of noon some 6,000 people had assembled before the scaffold.

The executioner was William Calcraft, who had come up from London to carry out the hanging. Shortly before midday he entered Burton's cell and pinioned his arms, then a procession led him to the 'drop'. As Burton had promised, he met his end with quiet dignity, ascending the scaffold with a firm step. Asked if he had anything to say, he declined, but tears were rolling down his face. He had just reached his nineteenth birthday. In his last moments he said, 'O Lord, remember me!' then the drop fell. Calcraft used the short drop which did not fracture the spine, so the condemned usually experienced the agonies of slow strangulation. Robert Burton, the man who wanted to be hanged, died without a struggle.

# 6

# THE UNWANTED WIFE

## *Cudham & Penge, 1877*

Harriet Richardson was born in 1841 and it must have been apparent from an early age that she would always need the care and protection of her mother. While physically robust, she was weak of intellect, often had outbursts of violent temper, and was unable to receive any more than the most basic education. Had Harriet been poor she would have lived out a long and uneventful life, but on the death of her aunt, Lady Rivers in 1872, she and her younger sister Ellen became entitled to a significant amount of money. Harriet's share was £2,500 with a reversionary interest (i.e. an interest in which she could not yet take possession) in other sums, the total of her fortune being about £4,300. (Sir Edward Clarke, writing about the case almost forty years later, stated that Harriet's mother was the illegitimate daughter of Eleanor Suter, mistress of Horace Pitt, Lord Rivers, whom she later married. Census records show that Lady Rivers was only three or four years older than Harriet's mother, who was also, before her marriage, a Miss Suter, and both were born in Brighton. It is more likely that they were sisters.) Harriet's mother, known as Mrs Butterfield since her second marriage to a clergyman, considered her mentally delicate elder daughter unsuitable for marriage.

In 1874 Harriet met Louis Staunton, ten years her junior, who was an auctioneer's clerk earning £1 a week. Louis set out woo Harriet and her money, but when Mrs Butterfield heard of their engagement she realised that her daughter was about to fall victim to a callous fortune hunter, and warned her not to marry. This only produced one of Harriet's rages, in which she threatened to kill her mother. In December Mrs Butterfield tried to have Harriet declared a lunatic, and place her money under the protection of the Court of Chancery, but she was unsuccessful, and on 16 June 1875 Harriet and Louis were married. Harriet's fortune, now the property of her husband, furnished a house at no. 8 Loughborough Park, Brixton, and the couple went to live there. Mrs Butterfield, trying to make the best of things, called on them in July, staying for only a few minutes, parting on friendly terms and saying that she would visit them again.

Louis Staunton had other ideas. Shortly after the visit Mrs Butterfield received a letter from him, telling her never to come there again. It enclosed a letter from her daughter, begging her not to call. What Mrs Butterfield did not know at the time was that Harriet was pregnant, having conceived probably in the first week of her marriage.

Louis' younger brother, Patrick Llewellyn Staunton, was a not very successful watercolour artist, who had married Elizabeth Ann Rhodes in 1873. There was a close bond between the brothers who saw each other often. Early in 1875 Patrick was living in Loughborough Park, opposite Louis, but in November that year Patrick and his family moved to Frith Cottage (later called Woodlands) at Cudham, Kent, an agricultural village seven miles from Sevenoaks with a population of about a thousand. Soon afterwards Elizabeth's sister, Alice, came to live with Louis and Harriet. Alice was a pretty girl of eighteen, and it was not long before Harriet noticed unwarranted familiarities between her husband and his sister-in-law, something which caused her considerable distress. As Harriet's confinement approached, Clara Brown, a sixteen-year-old maidservant, a cousin of Alice who had been in service with Patrick and Elizabeth since she was thirteen, joined the household. Clara soon noticed affectionate exchanges between Alice and Louis, and once found Alice's nightdress in a drawer in Louis' bedroom. On 23 March 1876 Harriet gave birth to a son, Thomas Henry Staunton. At the time of her confinement she was, in the words of her doctor, 'a perfectly well-nourished woman with large heavy cheeks' and weighed between 9½ and 10 stone. Although Harriet had plenty of milk, Louis said he did not want her to suckle the child. Emma Denton, a nurse who attended Harriet, commented that her charge 'frequently cried because her husband was always with Alice Rhodes.' At the end of April the baby, Tommy, was taken to Cudham by Alice and Louis, who returned to London leaving the child with Patrick and Elizabeth. Clara also joined the Cudham household.

If Clara was in any doubt about the relationship between Louis and Alice this uncertainly ended in the summer of 1876 when she found and read a letter in Louis Staunton's handwriting to Alice who had been staying at Cudham. According to Clara it read: 'It seems as though it never would be, but there will be a time when Harriet is out of the way, and we shall be happy together.' Not liking to admit she had seen the letter she burnt it. Alice, realising that the letter was not for prying eyes, searched for it, but when she asked Clara, the maid denied she had ever seen it.

By the end of August, Louis had decided that he wanted to live with Alice unhindered by his wife, and sent Harriet to live with his brother, supplying £1 a week for her keep. Harriet thought she was only visiting, and was unaware that her husband intended Cudham to be her permanent home. Woodlands was situated about 80 to 100 yards from the main road that passed through the village, and there was no carriage road leading up to the door, which had to be reached by crossing pasture. The cottage was small; it had two parlours downstairs, one 13ft 2in by

*Etching of a picture by Patrick Staunton. (Author's collection)*

12ft 10in, and one 13ft 2in by 8ft 2in, a kitchen and a cellar and above were two bedrooms, similar in size to the parlours. There were now four adults and three children living there – Patrick and his wife, and their two children, Harriet and her baby, and Clara Brown. Patrick, Elizabeth and one child occupied one bedroom, while Clara, Harriet and the two babies the other.

A month later Harriet wrote to Louis asking if she could come home, saying she had had no clean flannel in a month and her boots were worn out. It is not known if he replied. Even to Harriet's limited intellect it must eventually have dawned upon her that she was a prisoner. Patrick told Harriet she was not to go out of the house for anyone to see her, and Clara was ordered not to let Harriet out. When Harriet asked for her hat and jacket so she could go out she was told that Louis had taken them away with him. They had in fact been locked away in a box by Elizabeth, on Louis' orders. The only two occasions on which Harriet was permitted to leave Cudham were when she was taken to London to see a solicitor, Thomas Keene, regarding the sale and assignment of her reversionary interests. These visits were on the 17 and 23 October. On the second of these visits Keene noticed a bruise-like discoloration under one of her eyes, but did not like to ask about it.

Louis now had possession of everything Harriet had owned or to which she had been entitled. In October, he leased 22 acres of land and a house at Little Grays

Farm, Cudham, for £70 a year, and went to live there with Alice, who posed as his wife. The farm was about a mile from Woodlands, but was a very much more substantial property, having four bedrooms. It is probable that Harriet never knew of its existence.

During Harriet's stay in Cudham she was rarely seen except by the other occupants of the cottage. Neighbours and trades people called without even knowing that she lived there. Sometimes visitors heard a person moving about inside the house, and once Clara was heard to say 'Go back, Ma'am.' Two people had glimpsed her, including William Marchant, a gamekeeper, who had last seen her on 19 October. George Dewberry, who supplied corn and straw for the pony at Woodlands, did not see Harriet but heard a woman screaming on 22 October as if she was 'being roughly treated and knocked about.' He didn't think it necessary to report it.

*Little Grays Farm. (Author's collection)*

This was the day before Mr Keene noticed Harriet's black eye. One of the last sightings by someone not a member of the household was that of fishmonger John Staples, who saw Harriet on the Wednesday before Christmas, sitting in the kitchen with a child on her knees. She looked very ill.

When Harriet first went to live in Cudham she took her meals with the rest of the family, but just before Christmas this arrangement stopped. Harriet was kept in her room and food was sent up. It is not clear where Clara slept after this. Both Patrick and his wife told Harriet not to come downstairs as they did not want her there. Quite why this decision was taken is not known, but there was one urgent reason why Louis did not want to risk Harriet meeting anyone who might tell her about his life at Little Grays Farm. Alice had discovered that she was pregnant. At first Harriet was sent the same food as everyone else, but that too changed. Harriet found that she was not having enough to eat, and once, when she complained about this, Patrick struck her hard enough to bruise her arm. The room in which Harriet was kept was sparsely furnished and rarely cleaned. There was no carpet, and the bed consisted of a board laid between two trestles, with a dirty mattress and pillow. There was no basin or water jug. On some days Harriet was given no food at all, and as time passed she became thinner and weaker. The maintenance money from Louis must have been welcome to Patrick and Elizabeth, and keeping Harriet short of rations was a way of maximising their profit, especially as by the end of December Elizabeth would have known she was expecting her third child.

Was a conscious decision ever made to starve Harriet to death, or was it something that happened, unplanned and unacknowledged, starting with deprivation and cruelty and only gradually becoming intentionally lethal? Weeks went by, weeks during which Clara might have, but did not, report what was happening before her eyes, weeks in which Harriet's guardians could have, but did not, take action to ensure her survival.

Mrs Butterfield made frequent enquiries about her daughter's welfare, but it was not until a year after her visit that she discovered that Harriet and Louis were no longer in Brixton. The anxious mother made numerous attempts to trace her daughter, visiting members of the Rhodes family, and one of Louis' old servants, but no one could, or would, help. This may have prompted the letter which Louis sent to Mrs Butterfield on 20 January. In an effort to put her off the scent, the letter was headed 'Brighton'. He wrote, 'Now I tell you, once and for all, after your unnatural and brutal conduct to [Harriet] she never wishes to see you again, nor would I allow her to do so.'

In February Mrs Butterfield chanced to meet Alice Rhodes at London Bridge station, and asked where Harriet was. At first Alice claimed she did not know but when Mrs Butterfield insisted that she must do, Alice, claiming that she had not seen Louis for months, said that Harriet was in Brighton with her husband and baby. Mrs Butterfield noticed that Alice was wearing a brooch which had belonged to Harriet and was a particular favourite of hers. Challenged about this, Alice said that Harriet had given it to her.

On making further enquiries Mrs Butterfield learned that the Stauntons had moved to Cudham, and on 5 March determined to go there and make enquiries. On the way she saw Patrick at London Bridge station but when she asked where her daughter was he said, 'Damn your daughter, I know nothing about her.' When Mrs Butterfield said she would go to Cudham to find her, Patrick replied, 'If you do I'll blow your brains out, for I keep loaded firearms in the house.' Despite this, Mrs Butterfield went to Cudham, and asked if anyone knew where the Stauntons lived. From Elizabeth Uridge, the owner of Little Grays Farm, she learned that Louis Staunton was living there with his wife, and hired a fly to take her there. She was frightened of going there alone, but the coachman, George Wells, said that he would protect her. Louis and Elizabeth Staunton were there, and as the door opened and Mrs Butterfield walked in, Elizabeth tried to push her out, but the desperate mother forced her way into the house and asked Louis if she could see her daughter. He swore at her and said she could not. Mrs Butterfield pleaded with him – even if she could not speak to Harriet, she would like to hear her voice, or just see her hand on the baluster. Louis swore again, and said, 'you shall never see her if you live for a thousand years.' He picked up a knife and threatened to stab her, but Elizabeth begged him not to. She told Mrs Butterfield that her daughter was being well cared for and that that was enough for her to know. Louis and Elizabeth then elbowed and pushed Mrs Butterfield out of the house and shut the door. As the distressed woman returned to the waiting fly, the cabman pointed out the local doctor, Dr Creasey, who happened to be passing, and she spoke to him before she left, but learned nothing more. Mrs Butterfield next contacted the magistrate at Marlborough Street Police Court, who gave her a letter to take to the Sevenoaks police, to whom she gave all the information she had. Constable Alfred Holland of Knockholt suspected that Harriet was hidden either at Woodlands or Little Grays Farm, but despite keeping a frequent watch and making enquiries in the surrounding villages, was unable to confirm her whereabouts.

By the start of April, Harriet was probably too weakened by malnutrition to move without assistance. Little Tommy was also wasting away. He may well have been on the same regime of starvation as Harriet and had, according to Clara, been subject to violent abuse by Patrick. On Sunday 8 April, Patrick Staunton and his wife took the child to Guy's Hospital, saying that his mother was unable to care for him. Little Tommy was emaciated and too ill to take nourishment, and there was a bruise on his cheek. He died a few hours later. On 10 April, Louis Staunton, giving his name as John Harris and claiming to be a representative of the firm where the child's father worked, gave instructions for a cheap burial. The child was buried at Plaistow, in an unnumbered grave, and no relative attended.

In desperation, Revd Butterfield wrote to Alice and Elizabeth's mother, stating his belief that Louis was conducting an illicit relationship with Alice and asking where Harriet was. When Louis learned of the letter he responded saying he would take legal proceedings if he did not receive an apology, and threatened to report Revd Butterfield to his bishop and have Mrs Butterfield arrested if she tried to see

Harriet again. He did not mention the death of his son. On 9 April Mrs Butterfield applied to the Bromley magistrates for help, and consulted a solicitor.

The Stauntons, anxious to conceal Harriet's condition, and realising that the end was near, decided to move her to a location where the family was unknown, but she was by then so weak that it was uncertain if she could survive a journey. Attempts were made to feed her boiled fowl and sliced steak, which she was too ill to eat. On 11 April they tried her with bread and butter and milk, but she was unable even to manage that. On Thursday 12 April Louis and Elizabeth took lodgings in no. 34 Forbes Road, Penge, telling the landlady, Mrs Chalklin, that it was for an invalid lady who was able to eat but would not. They asked if she could recommend a good doctor and she suggested Dr Dean Longrigg. Later that day they called on Dr Longrigg, saying that they were bringing an invalid lady to live in Penge. Harriet was described as suffering from weak intellect and partial paralysis of the left side, 'clean in her habits' and 'thin but hearty.' Longrigg asked for the name of the medical man who had been attending the patient and found his informants evasive in their replies. Eventually, and reluctantly, they gave the name of Dr Creasey. There was no suggestion of any urgency, and he arranged to call on Harriet at 11 a.m. the following day. That same evening, Harriet was driven in a wagonette to Bromley station, from where she travelled by train with the Stauntons and Alice Rhodes. Harriet was too weak to walk or speak. She had to be lifted into a cab, and the only sound she made was groans.

At Forbes Road, Harriet was at once put to bed, and when Mrs Chalklin went up to see her she found the new tenant covered up to her face, making gurgling noises and moaning. The Stauntons made sure to allay any suspicions Mrs Chalklin might have had. The invalid, they said, had been well on the Saturday when she had enjoyed a nice steak with potatoes and turnip tops. Alice, who was wearing a wedding ring, and was obviously pregnant, was described as a married lady whose husband was away.

The following morning Alice called on Dr Longrigg to say the patient was much worse, and he went to see her at once. Harriet was unconscious, her arms rigid, pulse feeble, breathing shallow and laboured. Her face was 'fearfully shrunk', the balls of her eyes sunken into her head, the skin dry and a dirty brownish colour. Longrigg saw at once that she did not have long to live. He ordered beef tea and milk and arranged for a nurse, Ellen Gooding, to attend her. Nurse Gooding found the patient insensible, and attempted to feed her a spoonful of beef tea and a dose of medicine, as instructed, but Harriet was unable to swallow. Dr Longrigg returned at midday, and said that the patient was dying. At half past one, Nurse Gooding saw that the end was near. She went into the sitting room and, finding Louis and Elizabeth, asked Louis if he would like to see the last of his lady, but neither of the Stauntons came to the room. Harriet died a few minutes later.

When Louis was given the news he said nothing. Nurse Gooding tried to wash the body and found it caked with a layer of filth that was too encrusted to simply be wiped off with a flannel. She likened it to the bark of a tree. The hair, which had not been tended for some time, was alive with lice.

*Harriet Staunton on her bridal day and in her last hours. (Author's collection)*

On 14 April, based on information supplied by the Stauntons, Dr Longrigg gave a certificate that death was primarily due to cerebral disease and secondly, apoplexy. A funeral was quickly arranged to take place on the following Monday, the undertaker being asked that it should not cost too much. At that point it really must have seemed to the Stauntons that they had got away with it, but they were about to be undone by an extraordinary coincidence.

On Friday 13 April, Mr Louis Victor Casabianca, the husband of Harriet's sister Ellen, had chanced to be in a post office on Forbes Road when a young man came in with an enquiry. A death had occurred at a house in Forbes Road that morning, and since the road formed a boundary between Kent and Surrey, he was unsure where it would have to be registered. The young man (it was Louis Staunton) unwisely mentioned that the woman who had died had been brought there from Cudham. Mr Casabianca pricked up his ears. He knew that Mrs Butterfield had been asking about her daughter who had been living in Cudham. His enquiries revealed that the deceased lady was indeed his sister-in-law, and he spoke to Dr Longrigg, who withdrew his certificate and advised Casabianca to voice his suspicions to the police. Longrigg himself wrote to the coroner, saying that he had been called to 'a case of a somewhat peculiar character' and that from what he had learned after giving the certificate he thought there should be an inquest. One piece of information in Longrigg's letter must have hastened matters along. His postscript read 'The name of the deceased is Mrs Staunton, niece of Lord Rivers.'

Sergeant Joseph Bateman was sent to question the Stauntons. He spoke to Patrick, who claimed that Harriet had only been ill for a day or two and had eaten heartily up until then. He added when taken to Penge she had been well enough to walk and talk. Bateman found Patrick's manner suspiciously evasive. By order of the police, the funeral was postponed and a report was made to the coroner.

On 15 April Mrs Butterfield received a telegram telling her of the date and place of her daughter's death. It was not from any of the Stauntons, but from Mrs Uridge, the landlady of Little Grays Farm, with whom she had left her address on the March visit. Mrs Butterfield at once went to Forbes Road and saw Harriet's body in its coffin. She could hardly recognise her normally clean and healthy daughter, who was 'very dirty and looked very old and miserable.'

The inquest on Harriet Staunton, held at the Park Tavern, Penge, before the coroner Mr Carttar, opened on 18 April in the midst of considerable local excitement, fuelled by rumours that the deceased was a lady of fortune. Alice and the Stauntons arrived dressed in mourning. The *Sydenham Forest Hill and Penge Gazette* reported that if only a small portion of the circulating rumours were correct 'it will provide an exciting chapter of incidents that will read like some highly seasoned work of fiction!'

The post-mortem was carried out at Forbes Road on the following day in the presence of six doctors. The principal was Dr Longrigg, assisted by his partner Mr Piggott and a friend, Mr Lyster. John Edward Bright attended on behalf of Harriet's family, Mr Harman on behalf of Louis, and F.E. Wilkinson was the police surgeon. Harriet was 5ft 5¼in tall, but her emaciated body weighed just 5st 4lb. Her feet were filthy, with horny skin, showing that she had been without shoes for some time. There were lice both in the hair and on the body, which had been bitten. There were no marks of violence. The organs were small but healthy. There was a small amount of liquid, possibly tea or milk, in the stomach and a piece of bacon lodged at the back of the tongue. There were small tubercular deposits on the left lung and in the brain, but not enough to account for her condition. Some congestion of the brain and stomach suggested that she might have been poisoned, but later analysis was unable to detect any trace of poison.

All the Stauntons had given depositions stating that Harriet had been in good health until a few days before her death, and these statements were supported by Clara Brown. When the inquest resumed, Louis Staunton told the court that he had separated from Harriet by a private agreement due to her excessive drinking. He claimed that she had been well until the Monday before her death when she had complained of swollen feet. The next day she had felt worse but had said that she only had a cold, and on 12 April – the same day on which Harriet had been carried to Penge insensible and unable to speak – according to Louis' testimony when he asked her how she was, she replied 'pretty well.'

Elizabeth Staunton told the court that Harriet took her meals with the family and always appeared well until shortly before her death. She did not see her mother because she did not wish to. Patrick also stated that Harriet had been well up to

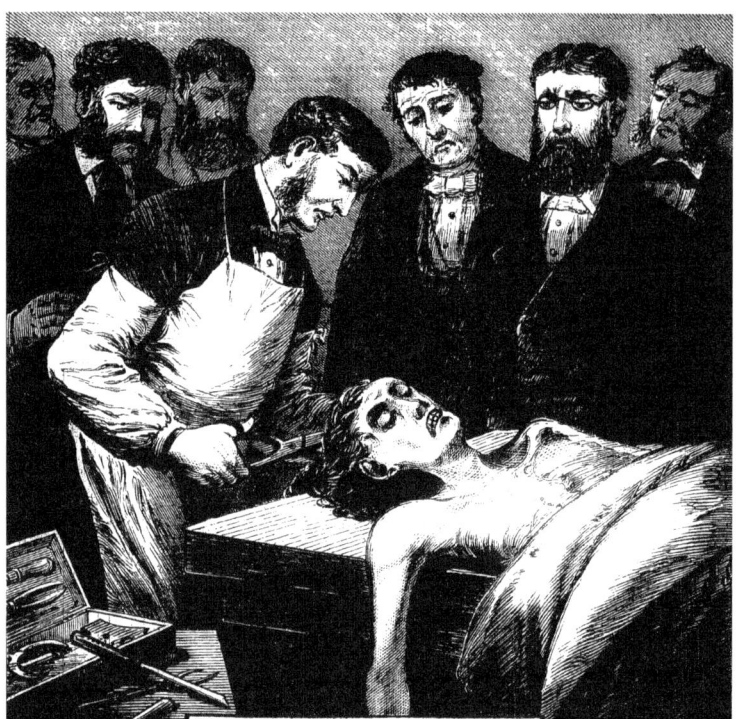

*The post-mortem examination. (Author's collection)*

the Monday before her death, and that he had frequently seen her intoxicated. Questioned by Mr Gye, who represented Louis, he said that Harriet had looked after her child herself and it had been well fed. She had always had money in her pocket and could come and go as she pleased. He added that there were no shops within half a mile of the house. Here the coroner interposed. 'I believe it is the wildest part of the county of Kent, and it would be worth your while, Mr Gye, to go and see it.'

A photograph of Harriet was produced in court, described as that of 'a comely stout woman'. Clara Brown gave evidence that on the Tuesday before her death Harriet had eaten cold roast beef for dinner, on the Wednesday hot fowl and on the Thursday steak, and her appetite had been good on each occasion. Dr Longrigg's description of the state of the body clearly demonstrated that the Stauntons, Alice and Clara had all been lying when they said Harriet had eaten recently. Neither was there any medical evidence to support the Stauntons' claim that Harriet had been a heavy drinker. Dr Russell, who had attended her in her confinement, said that Harriet did not drink, adding that her husband 'seemed to treat her with very great neglect.' Emma Denton testified to many occasions when Harriet had been ill-treated by her husband and Alice. The doctors felt that the removal to Penge had only accelerated death.

Although the inquest did not deal with the death of the child, the coroner felt it was relevant to the case and made sure to show the jury a copy of the child's death certificate, dated 3 May 1877. The cause of death was given as 'inanition' – exhaustion from lack of nourishment. As the facts emerged the public outcry became such that when the suspects were taken to and from the court police protection was required. Crowds milled around the courtroom making threatening gestures and shouting 'Lynch them!' At the close of the inquest the danger was so great that Alice and the Stauntons were advised not to be present.

On 19 March the inquest jury returned a verdict of wilful murder against all three Stauntons and Alice Rhodes. The cause of death was declared to be starvation. Alice and the Stauntons were placed under arrest and brought to Maidstone Gaol, where a large and angry crowd made a rush for their cab, obliging the terrified prisoners to run into the gaol.

It was not until 10 May that the police went to search Woodlands, still unoccupied since the Stauntons' arrest. They found that the front bedroom was properly furnished and clean, but the back bedroom, which had been occupied by Harriet and her son, was filthy, with no proper bed or washstand. Ten days later they went there again, and in the interim the back bedroom had been cleaned and furnished.

On 28 June Alice Rhodes gave birth to a son, Lewis Staunton Rhodes, in Maidstone Gaol.

At the Kent Assizes in July the grand jury found a true bill against all four prisoners, although it was pointed out by Sir James Stephen that Harriet had not been under the care of Alice Rhodes. On 28 July Elizabeth Staunton gave birth prematurely to twins, a healthy boy, Patrick Llewellyn Staunton, and a girl who died not long afterwards. Public feeling against the prisoners was so strong that the trial was removed to the Old Bailey, where it commenced on 19 September. The building was hot and crowded. Fashionable ladies in their best dresses and jewels attended every day, staring at the prisoners through opera glasses and lorgnettes. At lunchtimes they chatted eagerly with friends and refreshed themselves with champagne. The trial was presided over by Sir Henry Hawkins, only recently appointed to the bench. He later said it was his 'first and most sensational case', and he was determined to make his mark.

A crucial witness was Clara Brown. She had withdrawn her original statement, saying she had been coerced into it by her employers, and revealed to the court how Harriet had been treated.

The doctors were all firmly of the opinion that the cause of death was starvation, and that Harriet's condition at the time of her death would have taken about three months to produce. She had probably been too weak to walk for at least a week or two prior to death. The tubercular deposit on the brain was held to be the result of starvation, while the deposit on her lung had nothing to do with her death. There was no evidence that she was 'of intemperate habits'. There was hardly a trace of fat on the body and the severity of Harriet's condition must have been apparent to anyone who attended her. Independent witnesses who had seen Harriet on her last journey to Penge testified that she was helpless and almost insensible on the day before her death.

*The Stauntons and Alice after their arrest. (Author's collection)*

Edward Clarke, defending Patrick Staunton, did his best to suggest that death had been due to some cause other than starvation, but as was pointed out, even if Harriet had been suffering from a disease which had resulted in her loss of weight, why had no doctor been called until almost immediately before her death? Professor Rogers, a professor of toxicology, told the court, 'Most certainly, it must have been obvious to those who were about this lady that for some time before her death she required medical attendance.' Dr Longrigg must have suspected that his only function as far as the Stauntons were concerned was to provide a death certificate.

Dr Creasey, whom the Stauntons had told Longrigg was Harriet's medical man in Cudham, gave evidence that he knew the Stauntons, and had called at Woodlands on some trifling matters, but had never to his knowledge seen or attended Harriet or her child, or even known that they were living there.

Mr Montagu Williams, defending Louis Staunton, did his best to suggest that Harriet might have died from natural causes, as did Edward Clarke on behalf of Patrick. Mr Douglas Straight, defending Elizabeth Staunton, submitted that she could not be held responsible for Harriet's death as she must be presumed to have acted under the coercion of her husband. He elicited from Clara Brown that Patrick had been known to strike his wife in anger. Mr Gye, defending Alice Rhodes, stated that he did not believe there had been any case made against his client.

Mr Justice Hawkins' summing up commenced at twenty minutes to eleven on the morning of the final day, and with the occasional break, went on until twenty to ten that evening. The judge's views were clear from the outset. He made sure to read out a letter written by Alice to Louis in August 1876, which ended, 'Hoping I shall see my own darling soon, I remain your truly affectionate wife, Alice'. The postscript was 'I am not bad yet'. Clearly intimacy had taken place and Alice was waiting to see if she was pregnant.

Painstakingly, and in meticulous detail, the judge exposed the lies of Alice and the Stauntons, the blatant attempts to prevent Mrs Butterfield from seeing her daughter, the months of cruelty and neglect to which Harriet had been subjected. He was particularly scathing about the bruise on Tommy's cheek, and the fact that Patrick had hit the child; '... if he had much feeling or regard for the mother, one could hardly think that the blow would have been struck.'

The jury retired to consider their verdict and returned at five past eleven the same night. There was huge excitement in the still crowded court, and only with difficulty could some spectators be dissuaded from clambering on top of their seats for a better view. All four defendants were found guilty of murder, although the jury recommended both the women, especially Alice, to mercy. When she heard the verdict, Alice sobbed and was taken half fainting to the back of the dock, and placed in a chair. Louis was pale, and Patrick trembled and clasped Elizabeth's hand. She reassured him that she would be firm. When the verdict was relayed to the

*Mr Justice Hawkins (left) and the Home Secretary, Richard Cross. (Author's collection)*

crowds standing outside the court their loud cheers interrupted the solemn process of Mr Justice Hawkins pronouncing the death penalty. He described their crime as 'so black and hideous that I believe in all the records of crime it would be difficult to find its parallel.' He also stated that while they had not been convicted of the crime of murdering the child, he was satisfied in his own mind that they had contemplated, plotted and brought about his death. On hearing her fate, Elizabeth sank into a chair beside her sister, and Patrick silently pressed Louis' hand. Asked if they had anything to say, Alice wept that she was innocent. The press, like the public, greeted the verdict with approval and denounced the crime as 'revolting' and 'loathsome' and Louis as 'one of the most cold-blooded and heartless criminals that ever stood in the felon's dock.'

The executions were set for 16 October. In the condemned cells of Maidstone Gaol, Louis and Patrick were naturally despondent but the women were confident that they would not hang. Elizabeth stoutly maintained her innocence, asserting that Harriet could have had any food she chose, and the doctor had not been called earlier as she had not thought the illness was serious. She accused Clara Brown of having been influenced by Mrs Butterfield. Alice refused to discuss the case. Within days, Madame Tussauds was advertising a display of waxwork figures of Louis Staunton and Alice Rhodes.

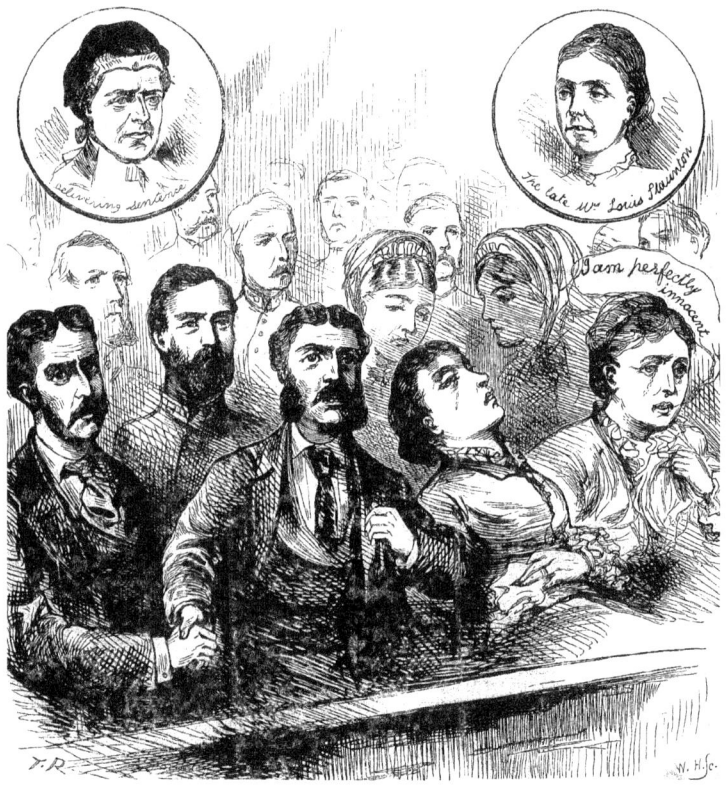

*The prisoners receive the sentence of death. (Author's collection)*

All through the trial the defence counsel had had a difficult case. The medical evidence had been clear, the defendants had obviously lied, and no one but they could have been responsible for Harriet's death. Yet one idea reverberated long after the verdict was given, the slight evidence of tuberculosis. The medical profession loved to get its teeth into a controversy and here was a golden opportunity. The pages of *The Times* were soon crowded with long letters from eminent doctors and surgeons, suggesting that the emaciation of the body might have been due in part, at least, to disease and not starvation. *The Lancet* weighed in stating that starvation as a cause of death was unproven, although there was overwhelming evidence that Harriet had been the victim of criminal neglect. The *British Medical Journal* believed that the facts should be carefully re-examined by the Home Office and urged reforms in methods of obtaining expert medical testimony. Further letters followed, claiming that patients with mental disease, even when well nursed, could be shockingly emaciated and dirty. The *Medical Examiner* urged that it was not fair for general practitioners to be called upon to give evidence on 'a subtle point of pathology.' On 9 October a 'very crowded, excited and somewhat noisy' public meeting was held at the Cannon Street Hotel for the purpose of approving a petition to the Queen to remit the sentences of death. Not all the attendees who thronged the Great Hall were in agreement however. In the chair, Mr Scarlet Campbell, a former Indian judge, declared that Harriet's condition was consistent with tuberculosis and dementia, and that she had not been neglected. Appealing to the meeting whether the case was one of starvation there were cries of both 'Yes!' and 'No!' A similar response greeted his question as to whether it was a case of murder. The petition was read and adopted by a substantial majority. Public excitement continued. Waxwork models of Patrick and Elizabeth joined those of Louis and Alice, and Patrick Staunton achieved some belated success as an artist when four of his paintings were put on sale at Maidstone.

On 12 October the Home Secretary held a long conference with several judges, professors of chemistry and medical men. Some of the trial witnesses, including Clara Brown, were questioned. The Home Office deliberations continued into the following day, and at 6 p.m. on 13 October a telegram was sent to the governor of Maidstone Gaol. The death sentences had been commuted. The news spread rapidly throughout the town, and large posters were put up outside newspaper offices where excited crowds gathered. The press had by now changed its view of the case. As *The Times* put it, 'we have had a very narrow escape of a miscarriage of justice.' All commentators deplored the fact that in that absence of a court of appeal, the turnaround in the case had relied upon a review by the publicly convened Cannon Street Committee and a further informal 'trial' at the Home Office. On 30 October the Home Secretary announced that the three Stauntons were condemned to penal servitude for life, but for Alice Rhodes there was a free pardon. Alice, it was felt, may have been the motive for the ill-treatment of Harriet, but in no sense was Harriet under her care. The question of Alice being an accessory, in that she had colluded with the Stauntons in concealing Harriet's location from her mother, was not considered.

*Respite of the convicts, prison life and dress at Maidstone Gaol. (Author's collection)*

After visiting her sister, Alice left the prison and took a train to London. What became of her later is unknown. As a result of the notoriety the case brought to Penge, Forbes Road was later renamed Mosslea Road.

Patrick and Louis were transferred to Woking Prison, where Patrick Staunton died of tuberculosis on 26 June 1881 aged twenty-seven. Elizabeth Staunton was confined to the Fulham Refuge, a reformatory women's prison in Burlington Lane, Chiswick. She was freed after a few years and according to Clarke (who was knighted in 1886), 'in another name found an occupation in which she made herself a prosperous position.' In 1897 Sir Edward was asked if he would be willing to meet Louis Staunton, recently released from prison. He agreed, and a middle aged man 'with subdued voice and gentle manner' came to his chambers. Louis, who had changed his name, wanted money to enable him to enter into business with a relative. Sir Edward gave him £100, and seven years later saw him again, in business for himself, married and with a child.

# 7

# THE VEILED LADY

## *Yalding, 1881*

Stephen Moore, a carpenter, and his wife Mary Elizabeth, both thirty-five years of age, had two children, Harry, born on 9 July 1873, and Georgina on 2 July 1874. Since 1876, the family had been living on the upper floor of no. 51 Westmoreland Street, Pimlico, where the landlady was a Mrs Caroline Rutter. Walter Clarke, a gardener, and his wife Eliza also lodged in the house. In 1878 Caroline's brother William Pay, a wheelwright, and his wife Esther, then both thirty-one, took over the property, and lived on the second floor. Esther, who had no children of her own, appeared to be very fond of Harry and Georgina – especially the little girl, whom she often used to take out, buying her toys and sweets.

In April 1881, the Moores moved to nearby no. 105 Winchester Street, but in October that year the couple separated. Mary and the children continued to live at Winchester Street and Stephen moved to Berkeley Street, Regent's Park. He still saw his family and on the morning of Tuesday 20 December he went there early to see his wife and children before going to work.

That morning, Georgina Moore went to school at 9.15 a.m., returning home to dinner at midday. Her meal included a hearty portion of currant pudding. Afternoon lessons were due to begin at 2 p.m., and the little girl went out to play at a quarter past one until it was time for school. When Georgina did not return home, Mary went to search for her, and finding that her daughter had not been to school that afternoon, sent a neighbour with a message to her husband at work. Stephen Moore spent the night searching for his daughter, visiting police stations and hospitals and questioning anyone who might have seen her.

One of Georgina's school fellows, seven-year-old Arthur Harrington, said that he had seen her in the company of a woman who wore a light-coloured Ulster cloak. The only woman Moore knew who wore such a garment was Esther Pay. Police Constable James Hill lived nearby and knew both families by sight. On the day of Georgina's disappearance he had seen the girl in Sutherland Street near Ebury

Bridge Road, Pimlico, with a tall, dark-haired woman in a black hat and light Ulster. He did not see the woman's face, but when he later heard that the child was missing he mentioned the incident to his inspector, saying he thought the woman might have been Esther Pay. On the Wednesday morning Mary went to see Esther, but she was not at home. Mary returned the following day, and this time Esther answered the door. When Mary asked if she knew anything about Georgina, Esther replied that she had not seen the child for a fortnight. Mary persisted that a little boy had seen her daughter with a woman in a light Ulster but Esther abruptly denied any knowledge, and shut the door.

*Suspicions of Esther Pay. (Author's collection)*

*Reward offered for missing girl. (Author's collection)*

GEORGINA MOORE,
THE LITTLE GIRL MISSING FROM PIMLICO.
[SEE £40 REWARD IN "LAW AND CRIME."]

Georgina's disappearance caused a sensation in Pimlico, and a reward of £5 was offered for her discovery. With rumours circulating that Esther knew something of the matter, it was impossible for her to remain aloof for long. That same Thursday Caroline Rutter's husband, James, visited Esther to talk about the mystery, and she also received a letter from Stephen Moore making an appointment to meet her at Charing Cross on Friday.

When Esther saw Stephen he asked her if she had heard the stories that she was supposed to know something about Georgina. Esther said she had, but at the time of the child's disappearance she had been out shopping with Caroline Rutter.

On 29 December the matter was handed over to Inspector Marshall of Scotland Yard. He called on Esther at Westmoreland Street on 5 January together with Stephen Moore. Esther insisted she knew nothing about the child's disappearance, maintaining that on the day in question she and her sister-in-law had been visiting shops in the King's Road and Fulham. The inspector cannot have been satisfied with this story as he returned the following day saying, 'I thought I had better see you alone.' As Esther continued to deny any involvement he heard a voice in the adjoining room. 'That is my husband,' said Esther, 'and he thinks you are Moore and you had better leave.' Moore, she explained, had been forbidden to enter the house.

When Marshall questioned the Clarkes he was told that on the day Georgina disappeared they had been busy preparing to move to new lodgings. Esther had told Eliza she was going out to the Aquarium (the Royal Aquarium was a popular place of entertainment) with Mrs Harris at 4 o'clock that day but would be back by seven. Eliza asked Esther, who was wearing her Ulster, to look after her children while she did some shopping. She went out at half past twelve and returned just fifteen minutes later, to find that her landlady had gone. When her husband came home they spent the rest of the day moving their possessions. She finally cleaned the rooms and left at half past nine, having seen no further sign of Esther. The next morning between nine and ten she returned to pay the last of the rent, but after knocking several times, got no answer. It was twenty past one when Esther came to see Eliza and told her the news that little Georgy had been lost. Esther said she had got home at ten the previous night after getting very wet. She had been with a friend, Mrs Harris at the aquarium, and then with Mrs Rutter. Marshall next interviewed Caroline Rutter, who confirmed Esther's alibi.

More than a week after Georgina's disappearance, Esther began to show some signs of anxiety about the child. She began calling on Mary Moore to ask about her, and sending her notes, and almost every day she called on Stephen for news. Days became weeks, and there was no sign of the little girl.

On 15 January 1882, James Humphrey, Esther's uncle, who was employed at Kenward's Farm, Yalding, found a hat hanging on a willow bough on the banks of the River Medway. There was no reason for him to attach any suspicion to it, and it was so dilapidated that he simply hung it on a bush.

In Pimlico, the marriage of Esther and William Pay collapsed in a welter of suspicion. On 25 January Esther left her husband and went to live in lodgings in Lower Sloane Street under the name of Black. Three days later she travelled by train to her parents' house at Nettlestead, a village about five miles from Maidstone on the banks of the Medway. Stephen Moore saw her off at the station. On arrival she wrote a friendly note to him saying he must tell her if there was any news of 'your little Georgy'.

On Monday 30 January, some 700 yards from the home of Esther's parents, waterman Alfred Penhorn was steering his barge near Hampstead Lock on the Medway, a point just a few minutes' walk from Yalding railway station, and only 15 yards from where a footpath towards the Humphreys' house branched off from the towpath. The vessel was some 10ft off its course, and he was trying to force it back with a boom when the hook caught in something at the bottom of the river. Bringing the object to the surface, he saw to his horror that it was the decomposed corpse of a child.

Stephen Moore was brought to view the body and identified it as that of Georgina. The post-mortem was carried out by Dr Bond of London and Dr Wood of Yalding. The body was covered with blue clay and the hands were clenched. Around the chest were several coils of wire fastened in a knot, and attached to the wire was a fire-brick, stamped 'Tyne'. There was a dark mark on the front of the neck extending from the root of the tongue to the breast-bone. The lungs did not contain any water and the stomach was full of undigested food. From the stomach contents it was apparent that Georgina had died on the day she had disappeared. The cause of death was strangulation from pressure over the larynx. There was no doubt that the child had been murdered.

Shown the clothing found on the body, Mary Moore identified it as that worn by her daughter on the day she disappeared. She believed that the child had not been undressed as the strings looked exactly as she had tied them.

On 31 January a man called Large saw a black woollen scarf on the bank of the Medway, only 2½ yards from where the body had been found. It was half in the

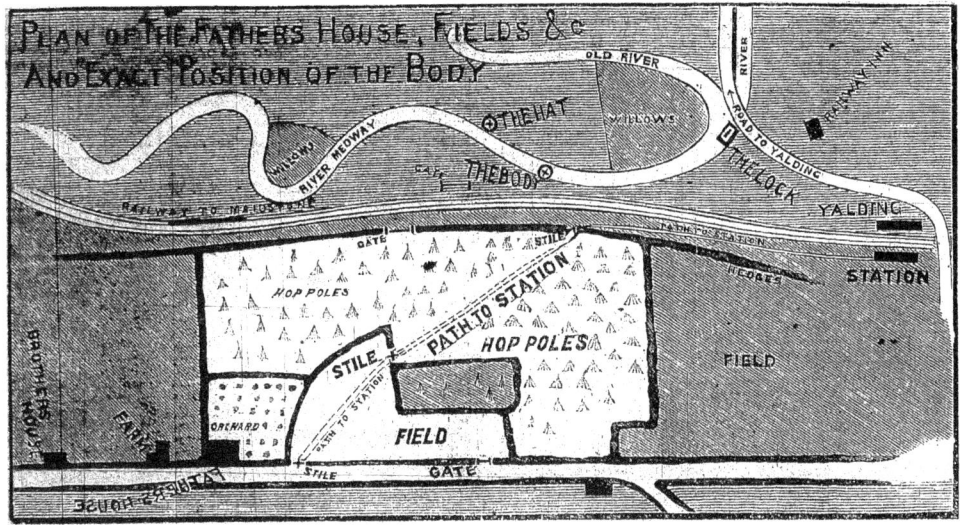

Map showing father's house and where the body was found. (Author's collection)

water, caught in a bush, and he reached it out with a stick. Realising it might be of importance he handed it to a local policeman who washed it. It was shown to Mary Moore who did not recognise it.

On the same morning Inspector Marshall, accompanied by Sergeant Cussens, went to the Humphreys' cottage at Yalding, and told Esther he wanted to see her about the child again. Esther said that she knew nothing about Georgina's disappearance.

'Have you not heard that yesterday a child was found in the Medway at the back of your house?' he asked, to which she replied 'No.' It was extremely unlikely that anyone in the little village could have been unaware of this tragic event, yet Esther stuck determinedly to her story. Marshall told her that he was detaining her on suspicion of stealing the child and that she might well be charged with causing her death. 'Well, you must prove it,' she said. 'I brought nothing with me but a birdcage, a bag and a small parcel.'

Marshall searched the cottage, and Esther's bag, which contained a recent issue of the *Penny Illustrated Paper* with a picture of Georgina, the rent book and keys of Esther's home, a sheet of notepaper which had marks on it that looked like blood, and a letter to Stephen Moore.

Marshall told Esther that her husband had been telling people she was implicated in Georgina's death, to which she replied, 'Don't you believe it.' At 10 a.m. Esther was taken to Yalding railway station and left in charge of Sergeant Cussens while Marshall went to make further enquiries. James Humphrey handed him the hat he had found, which was identified as Georgina's. It was later calculated that the hat had been found 292 yards from the body, and must have drifted down the stream, washed there by a heavy flood that had taken place on 12 January. Marshall was also handed the black scarf found in the water.

*Esther's father's house. (Author's collection)*

While they waited, Esther asked Cussens where the body had been found, and when he told her it was near to her father's cottage she said that was strange as the only people who knew her address there were her husband and the Moores. She told him that Moore was 'very artful' and she would not be surprised if he soon went missing. 'He is not on very good terms with his wife, and now he has got rid of Georgy you had better look very sharp after him.' She then offered to give the police the names of women Moore had been intimate with, who she said ought to be enquired into. Whoever did it, she added, knew where her home was and brought the child there to plant the murder on her. When Marshall joined them at 3 p.m. Esther asked if Moore was there. On being told he was she demanded to see him, but Marshall would not allow it, neither would he agree to let Esther and Moore ride in the same railway carriage. Annoyed, Esther said, 'Well don't you feel surprised if he bolts, and then you will find that the most guilty party has gone.' On the way up to London Esther said:

> This child has been killed out of spite to Moore, for he has served women very badly, some that I know worse than me, and he has served me badly enough. Why don't you discover them? Then you may get on the right track.

As an afterthought she added, 'One can only die once, and I shall not die a coward.'

At Westminster police station Esther was confronted with Moore, who told her that he had believed her to be innocent until the body was found so near to her house, and now he believed her to be implicated.

'How can you say so?' she replied, 'Mind this is not the means of your own character being investigated, which may bring out something you may not like.' She stared at him defiantly as she spoke, while he, throughout the whole meeting, was unable to look her in the face. She was charged with murder.

Inspector Marshall decided to hold an identity parade. Little Arthur Harrington walked along a row of thirteen women, and when he came to Esther made a dead stop. He walked along the line, then came back and pointed to Esther, saying she was the woman he had seen with Georgina. Constable Hill also identified Esther as the woman he had seen on 20 December.

The police had traced a boy employed at an ironmonger's shop in Pimlico, who said he had sold a firebrick like the one attached to the body to a woman shortly before Christmas, but he was unable to identify Esther as the customer.

On 1 February, Esther Pay was charged at the Westminster Police Court on suspicion of causing the death of Georgina Moore. The magistrate, Mr Partridge, asked her if she had any professional assistance, to which she replied she did not, and on being asked if she wanted any she said she did not need any help. It was a note of truculent defiance. When the hearing resumed on 8 February the prosecutor was the renowned criminal lawyer Mr (later Sir) Harry Bodkin Poland. A young solicitor, Mr Thomas Duerdin Dutton, represented Esther.

One of the most confusing pieces of evidence in the case was the scarf found in the Medway. Eliza Clarke had sworn that it was one she had seen Esther making and later wearing, but Inspector Marshall had taken a mauve scarf from Esther's house, and confronted with it in court, Eliza then thought that this was the one she had seen Esther with.

Caroline Rutter had withdrawn her alibi statement as soon as the child's body was found, and it was revealed that Esther had attempted to establish an alibi long before Georgina's fate was known. Early in January, Esther had told James Rutter that Inspector Marshall had asked her where she was on the day Georgina disappeared. Esther said she remembered the day very well. 'I told him I was along with Carrie (Caroline Rutter) and we went for a walk to see the shops in the King's Road and Fulham.' She told James, 'When you go home mind you tell Carrie to say the same.' When James went home he passed the message on to his wife. Esther had later told Caroline, 'If anyone comes up and asks you where I was, tell them I was out with you looking at the shops about Fulham, King's Road, and Hammersmith.' Caroline naturally asked why she should say this, and Esther said, 'I was with Mrs Harris, and we had a spree on, but I do not want her to get into a row.' Caroline accepted the explanation and when she was initially questioned by Inspector Marshall she supported Esther's story. The finding of the body so close to the home of Esther's parents had radically changed the position; Caroline told the court that she had not seen Esther at all on 20 December, and Mrs Emma Harris, a forty-seven-year-old wife of an unemployed joiner who lived at no. 71 Hugh Street, testified that neither had she.

Georgina was buried on Saturday 3 February. Her body had been returned to her mother's home in Winchester Street, and a crowd of some 2,000 assembled outside. The coffin was placed in an open car, and as Stephen Moore appeared and took his place in a mourning coach, it was apparent that a great fury had arisen against him, for the people groaned and hissed at him. Some demonstration must have been anticipated as there was a large force of police present headed by two inspectors, who had some difficulty in protecting him from the violence of the mob, and a cordon of constables was formed around the vehicle. In this way the cortège moved off towards Brompton Cemetery, the crowds increasing as they went, with noisy demonstrations. The scene in the cemetery was described as 'shocking and scandalous', and so violent was the crowd that the police had to lock Moore into the mortuary chapel for his own protection. He was unable to go to the grave or return with the other mourners, and was not released until after dark when the crowd had dispersed.

Questioned before the magistrates on 15 February, the confusion of Eliza Clarke about the scarf became all too apparent. She remembered Esther making a scarf and there had been some dispute at the time as to whether the colour was mauve or violet. The scarf found in the river was so dark blue as to be almost black, but Eliza said it was the same one but darkened by the water. She said it had the same size holes in the stitch, although was willing to admit it could have shrunk in the river. Mr Dutton then produced a roll of bright mauve wool which Eliza examined and said it was the same colour as the scarf she had seen Esther make. He then handed her an unfinished mauve scarf with a skein of wool attached which had been found at the Humphreys' house and asked Eliza if that was the scarf she had seen Esther make. After some hesitation she said it was. He now produced the scarf found in the river and asked if she could still swear that it was the one she had seen Esther making. 'I'm afraid I can't', she said. Mr Poland asked her about a black scarf that Esther used to wear, and Eliza said Esther had made a black one with the same stitch, but the damage to the prosecution case had been done.

On 20 February the inquest resumed at Yalding and the jury brought in a verdict of 'wilful murder' against Esther Pay, who was committed to trial at the assizes.

The police had been enquiring after anyone in the Yalding area who might have seen Esther and Georgina on 20 December, and further witnesses were emerging whose evidence suggested that Esther had been there on that day. The approaching Christmas season, and other local events had helped them fix the date of the sightings. Paddock Wood is about three miles south west of Yalding, and Charles Barton, a fly-proprietor (a fly was a light carriage), had seen a woman and a little girl walking from Paddock Wood station shortly before Christmas. A few days before Christmas Charles Cronk, an ostler, had been in the Kent Arms at Paddock Wood and had seen a woman pass by with a child. A labourer at Judd's Corner had also seen a woman and

*The George Inn, Yalding, where the inquest was held. (Author's collection)*

a child walking from Paddock Wood. None could positively identify Esther. Hannah Prout, landlady of the Queen's Head, Queen Street, Brenchley (a village between Paddock Wood and Yalding) said that on the Tuesday before Christmas a woman came into the tavern and asked for some gin. She was wearing a veil, carrying a little parcel and seemed very 'jolly'. Understandably, Hannah was unable to identify Esther. Stephen Bawden had been in the Queen's Head on the same day, and had seen a woman whom he believed was the woman in the dock. George Waghorn, a beer-house keeper, had also been there and saw the same veiled woman. Although no child had been with the woman in the tavern, Waghorn had seen that when the woman went out she had a child with her as she passed the window. Robert Bullard, a brickmaker, did not see the woman in the house but saw her with a little child outside. The woman and child had walked in the direction of Yalding.

Thomas Judd, formerly landlord of the New Inn, Yalding, near Lattenford, almost a mile from the Queen's Head, and less than three miles from where the body was found, said that on Tuesday 20 December a woman came into his tavern with a little girl at about 6 o' clock. She had two pennyworth of sweet biscuits and gave one to the little girl. It was a nasty drizzly night and the woman wore a veil but had kept it up and had not tried to conceal her features. Judd was shown a photograph of Georgina and thought it was very like the little girl he had seen. The woman had stayed there about half an hour and had some whisky. He noticed the child had a woollen shawl over her shoulders and was very tired. Judd had not given the matter any thought until he had been visited by a constable on 12 March. He was unable to make any positive identification.

Mrs Kemp, a wagoner's wife, knew the Humphreys. On 21 December she and her aunt had travelled from Yalding to Maidstone to do her Christmas shopping, and at Yalding station she had seen Mrs Humphrey with another woman, who was leaning on a fence with her hands to her head. She heard Mrs Humphrey call her companion 'Esther'. The younger woman mentioned that she had been twelve years married and had no children. Joining in the conversation, Mrs Kemp asked Mrs Humphrey what was the matter with her daughter, to which the reply was that she did not like to go home as her husband used her badly.

The only evidence Mr Dutton offered in Esther's defence was that of her parents. William Humphrey was seventy-three. He had been in the service of Mr White, a hop-grower of Nettlestead Court, for fifty-one years and had been a bailiff for forty-five. He said he had seen his daughter in August 1881, and after had that she had not visited him until the Saturday before her arrest. Mary Humphrey, Esther's mother, confirmed this account. Esther was committed for trial on a charge of murder.

On 12 April it was reported in the newspapers that a soldier named Reuben had given himself up to the police in Kildare, Ireland, saying that he was with Esther Pay when Georgina was murdered, but this line of enquiry must have come to nothing.

The hearing opened at Lewes on 26 April 1882 before Mr Baron Pollock. Mr Poland prosecuted, assisted by Robert Biron, but in the interim Esther had obtained a very substantial asset, defence counsel Edward Clarke. Clarke was the master of the dramatic speech with which he was known to move juries to tears, and he left no avenue unexplored to defend his clients. Although he could command a substantial fee, he was willing to take on difficult or high-profile cases for little or nothing if he felt they would enhance his reputation.

In the hearings that had taken place thus far no motive had been offered for the crime, but in his opening address Mr Poland revealed that an 'improper intimacy' had arisen between Esther and Stephen Moore while he had been living at Winchester Street, and this had continued until June 1881 when he broke off the relationship and went to live with another woman in Berkeley Road, Regent's Park. Poland suggested that Esther had killed the little girl to revenge herself upon Moore for deserting her. The court must have looked hard at Esther at that point. What sort of woman, the jury must have asked themselves, would kill an innocent child for such a reason?

Esther, described by the *East Sussex News* as 'fine-looking and well-dressed', was not an easy woman to like. Her demeanour in court was 'rather that of a spectator than of a prisoner under trial for murder. She was perfectly calm and collected, and was observed to smile occasionally.' On one occasion, when Clarke said something that unintentionally caused some smiles in court, she 'laughed so heartily that I sent her word by the solicitor that her demeanour was making my task much harder.'

Poland suggested that Esther had taken the child by train from Charing Cross to Paddock Wood, and had avoided waiting at the station for the Yalding train as she thought she might be recognised. Finding that the hire of a fly would cost 4s,

*Esther Pay in the Police Court. (Author's collection)*

compared with the rail fare of 3*d*, she had decided to walk. The woman with the child had been seen at Lattenford at about 6.30 p.m. and could well have reached Yalding by half past seven. A witness stated that he had heard a child's cry sometime between 7 and 8 p.m. at Yalding. The prosecution case was that Esther had prepared for the murder by buying the firebrick, and this was in the parcel the veiled woman had been carrying. The wire was some 7 or 8ft in length, and had been carefully twined around the brick and then the child's neck. Mr Poland said that Esther had not returned to her home that night but in all probability had spent the night with her parents, and had been seen the next morning with her mother at Paddock Wood railway station.

When Stephen Moore took the stand he found that Esther's threat that things might be revealed about him he wanted to remain secret was no idle comment. He admitted that he had formed an immoral connection with Esther while living in Westmoreland Street and the relationship had continued for six weeks after he left. He broke off the relationship because William Pay had seen him talking to Esther and 'it caused some unpleasantness.' According to Clarke's later account of the case, Pay had been violent to his wife. In October Moore had gone to live with a married woman, who passed as his wife. On 20 December he had been working all day until half past eight at night. He elaborated on the conversation he had had with Esther on 24 December, and revealed something he had never said under previous questioning. Some six months before he had left Westmoreland Street there had been a falling out between them and Esther had threatened, 'I will steal Georgy from you.' He had assumed at the time that she had only said it as a joke.

The court was naturally sympathetic to the plight of the father, but it was essential for Clarke to expose the defects in the witness's character. Even if there was no possibility that Moore had been involved in the crime (his work time-sheets produced in evidence provided an unshakeable alibi), the jury would be less likely to trust his statements implicating Esther if they regarded him as a rogue. Clarke also wanted to explore the accusation made by Esther, that there were many other women who had grudges. Under cross-examination, Moore was obliged to admit that when he had gone to identify the body of his daughter he had been accompanied by Mrs Maidment, the woman with

*The witnesses in court. (Author's collection)*

*Stephen Moore. (Author's collection)*

whom he was living. He admitted that he had not married Mary Elizabeth until after their son Harry was born, and when asked if he had been married before, refused to answer on the grounds that it might incriminate him. He admitted that when he lived at Bath he had been going under the name of Harry Williams and had been intimate with a Mrs Irwin, who had borne him a child. One of her sisters, Alice Day, had charged him with being the father of her child. Asked if he knew a young woman named Carroll he squirmed under the questioning and eventually admitted he had 'walked out' with her, up to December 1881. His wife had not known where he went when he was out. Clarke tasked him with the fact that he had never before mentioned Esther's threats to steal the child. Finally, Clarke showed that Moore still had a fondness for Esther. 'I did not suspect her but other people did,' he said. 'I had no reason to wish her away from London ... I had no ill-feeling towards Mrs Pay when I discontinued seeing her; it was on account of her husband. Down to that time we had been on the most affectionate terms.'

Moore said he did not know where either Mrs Irwin or her sister was on 20 December, although Miss Carroll was then away in Yorkshire. None of these ladies had any connection with Yalding or knew Georgina.

Mary Elizabeth Moore took the stand, and wept bitterly at the loss of her child. Georgina, she said, had been a timid child who would not have gone away with a stranger. She had not known about her husband's intimacy with Mrs Irwin or that he had once called himself Harry Williams, until that lady had told her about it. Letters had come to the house addressed to Harry Williams, and Alice Day had visited asking after her husband. In 1875 she had taken the two children and gone to stay with her father for a time. She had never heard of Mrs Maidment, but her husband used to go out night after night and she never knew where he went.

Little Arthur Harrington gave evidence, saying that he had picked out Mrs Pay in the line-up by the Ulster she wore. He had not known her previously. Before the court adjourned for the day Mr Clarke said he wanted the jury to examine the wire and the brick. There was a length of 2 or 3ft of wire between the brick and the coil round the body which he particularly wanted them to see.

In court a surveyor gave the distances the woman and the child had covered – from Paddock Wood station to the fly stables, then the Kent Arms, the Judd's Corner, the Queen's Head, the New Inn, to Saltingdon near Yalding and finally to the point where the body was found, a total of 5½ miles. The distance from the place where the body was found to the house of the man who had heard the cry was 200 yards.

Clarke cross-examined the witnesses who reported seeing the veiled lady and the child on 20 December in an effort to shake them about the date of the sighting, but with only limited success. Most, especially the Judds, were certain about the date. Mrs Kemp, who said she had seen Esther and her mother at Yalding station on 21 December, was a problem for the defence. Clarke tried to suggest that she was confusing this meeting with the last time Esther had been at Yalding on August bank holiday 1881, but Mrs Kemp was adamant that she had only ever met the two women together once, and it was just before Christmas. Her aunt corroborated her story.

Eliza Clarke's confusion about the scarf may not have been useful to the prosecution, but she had detailed information about Esther's movements on 20 December. Esther had later told her that Inspector Marshall had been to see Mrs Rutter. Anxious as to what her sister-in-law might have told the police, she claimed that Mrs Rutter was drunk when interviewed, saying, 'God knows what she may have said about me; and I believe between them they will hang me.' Eliza also told the court that about a year previously she had heard Esther say that Moore was a bad man and that she would either 'stick' him or shoot him, she could not remember which.

A joiner named Lang, the man who Mary had sent to tell her husband of Georgina's disappearance and who had helped Stephen search for his daughter, had been told by Mrs Pay that she was sorry for Mrs Moore but that 'it served Moore d****d well right.' He had told her he believed she knew more about the child's disappearance 'than any breathing soul.'

Mrs Harris gave evidence that there had been an arrangement to go to the Aquarium on 13 December but she had been unable to go. She had never been to the aquarium with Mrs Pay on that day or any other, and had not seen her at all on the 20th. Caroline Rutter said she had not been with Esther on 20 December. Clarke, in an effort to introduce an alternative suspect, asked her about her brother, William Pay, and elicited the admission that she could not describe him as a sober man and he had a violent temper.

Mr Poland was anxious to show that other potential suspects had alibis and was able to bring evidence that both Stephen Moore and William Pay had been at work during the afternoon and evening of 20 December.

The strongest witnesses in Esther's favour were her own family. Her parents, who believed in her innocence with a moving fervour, were adamant that Esther had not visited them on 20 December. Mrs Humphrey said that she and Esther had seen Mrs Kemp at the station on the August visit, and that Mrs Kemp was mistaken about seeing her on the morning of 21 December. Esther's father, brother and sister stated in corroboration that Mrs Humphrey had been unwell and had not left the house in the week before Christmas.

It was now up to Mr Clarke to make one of his famous speeches, and he did not disappoint. He reminded the jury that their decision was one of life or death and a mistake would be irrevocable. The crime of which Esther was accused 'was too barbarous for a woman to commit' and she would have needed 'superhuman strength' to throw the body, weighted with a brick, into the river. Only a man could have both the nerve and physical strength to commit the crime, deliberately leaving a length of wire between the body and the brick so the body would come to the surface and throw suspicion on his client. The choice of 20 December for the crime, the date on which the Clarkes were leaving, was, he represented, absurd, and the whole theory of Esther's supposed movements improbable. There was no adequate motive for such a deed, and nothing connected Esther to the crime. Clarke suggested that the murder had not been committed at Yalding at all, but in Pimlico. He believed that Esther's story about having been in the company of Mrs Rutter on 20 December to be true, and that Mrs Harris had been mistaken about the date. The evidence of the witnesses who said they had seen the veiled lady at Yalding was 'imperfect and unsatisfactory' – most did not recognise the woman and 'became practically witnesses for the defence'. On the other hand, the prisoner's family was correct about Esther not having visited them in December.

In summing up, the judge attached considerable importance to the evidence of Judd who he said seemed 'an honest and intelligent witness.' He referred to Esther's threats to steal the child, and the fact that Georgina would not have accompanied a stranger. Esther's statements about having been with Mrs Rutter and Mrs Harris, denied by those ladies, were 'a grave matter for the jury to consider.' Were the stories to conceal guilt, or merely to avert suspicion? The jury would also have the difficult task of reconciling the evidence of the prisoner's parents, undoubtedly respectable people, with that of Mrs Kemp.

The jurymen retired, but were absent only a short while. They delivered a verdict of 'not guilty' which was, according to *The Times*, 'received with some applause.'

Esther, unable to restrain her feelings of joy, bowed to the jury with an almost inaudible 'thank you' and left the court by the back door to avoid the crowds at the front.

In the following year Esther and William Pay were divorced on the grounds of Esther's adultery with Stephen Moore, and William remarried. Esther went into service in a public house where, initially, her presence attracted some attention. According to Clarke, however, she 'drifted downwards, and some time later was sent to prison for stealing blankets from a room in which she lodged.' A few years later, Mr Poland's associate, Robert Biron, now a QC, was prosecuting a murder case at Kingston Assizes, when he noticed a good-looking woman in court who smiled and nodded when she caught his eye. She was Esther Pay, and spoke to him when the case was over. He asked her why she was there and she replied, coolly, 'Oh, I thought I should like to hear another murder trial.'

Mary Moore was not reunited with her husband. In 1901 she was living with her son, Harry. Both Stephen Moore and Esther Pay may well have decided to adopt aliases. Their eventual fate is unknown.

# 8

# THE MYSTERIOUS DEATH OF DR LYDDON

## *Faversham, 1890*

The ancient market town of Faversham has a prominent place in the history of true crime. The murder of merchant Thomas Arden by his wife and her lover in 1551 was immortalised in the play *Arden of Faversham* published in 1592; one of the great Elizabethan classic dramas, it is still performed today. More mysterious, however, and far less well known is the death of Dr William Reeks Lyddon in 1890.

Lyddon was born in Hayfield, Derbyshire in 1849, the son of John Lyddon, a collector of taxes, and his wife Eliza. William's mother died when he was a year old. In 1870 John married Elizabeth Twort, an innkeeper's widow with two sons and a daughter, Sarah. In 1861 the Lyddons were living in West Malling, Kent, when Elizabeth gave birth to William's half-brother, Charles. In 1872 William, by then a qualified doctor, married Sarah Twort, and early in 1878 he established himself as a general practitioner at no. 12 West Street, Faversham. The couple's happiness was to be short-lived, for Sarah died in the summer of that year, aged twenty-seven. William was devastated by the loss, and kept many treasured mementoes of his wife.

Charles Lyddon was then a medical student living with his parents in Canterbury, but from July 1878, he began working for his brother in the dispensary attached to the practice, travelling back and forth from Faversham to do so. It was agreed that he would be paid £50 a year for his services, but William, who always seemed to be short of money, never paid him a penny, and even borrowed from Charles. Charles was able to keep himself, as he had an allowance from his parents, but it was clearly an unsatisfactory state of affairs. William's money problems may have been partly due to an addiction to alcohol, which may have been precipitated or intensified by the death of his wife. His drunkenness not only consumed the profits of his practice but made him unreliable and sometimes unable to work.

John, Elizabeth and Charles Lyddon eventually went to live with William in Faversham, where John Lyddon died in 1886. Mrs Lyddon also drank to excess, but Charles had developed a drink habit that exceeded even that of his brother. While William would consume about half a pint of whisky a day, Charles regularly drank more than a pint. Frequently drunk, sometimes incapable, Charles never completed his medical studies, and was casting an envious eye on his half-brother's valuable property and practice. As William entered his forties he was a thin, pale man, in a poor state of health due to alcoholism and self-neglect, and Charles saw to his concern that the practice was declining in value.

In April 1889 William was about to go into St Thomas' Hospital for an operation on a fistula, and was afraid that he might not survive. His debt to Charles was by then £560 for ten years' unpaid salary and a loan. William had not made a will, and Charles, concerned that he might lose his interest in the debt if William died, persuaded his brother to sign a deed of assignment before he went into hospital. The deed was drawn up on 1 May 1889 by Mr F.G. Gibson, a solicitor of Sittingbourne.

Under this deed, William agreed to sell and assign to Charles all his interest and goodwill in the practice, its debts, stock, furniture, carriages, horses, plate and effects, for the sum of £560. The deed was signed by both brothers in the presence of neighbour Richard Dunn, landlord of the Sun Inn at next door no. 10. George Adam Amos, who was then coachman to the Lyddons, was also present at the signing. William was led to believe that if he survived surgery the deed would be set aside, but on the following day he was already regretting what he had done, and told Amos that the deed had been made in 'a very foolish manner'. Charles, who had been celebrating his new situation with his customary several drinks, came up and ordered William to go into the surgery where a patient was waiting. As his brother departed, Charles drew the paper from his pocket and told Amos, 'I am master of everything now.' He added that he must stop William drawing money from the bank where there was a sum of £5,000 held jointly by the three Lyddons.

William had been taking morphia for the pain of the fistula, and was also given some in hospital. Unexpectedly, he made a good recovery from the surgery, and pronounced himself pleased that he had been able to break the morphia habit. On returning home, he asked his brother for the deed, but Charles refused, saying that he was now the master and henceforward, any money taken in the practice belonged to him.

Until that time, relations between the brothers had been amicable, but from then onwards there were frequent quarrels and violent episodes. 'Charles was always on to his brother and knocking him about,' reported Amos, who had seen Charles punch William, blackening his eye, and knocking him against the bedstead where he bruised the back of his head. Amos also saw Mrs Lyddon hit William with a stick, bruising his arm. One night Charles ordered Amos up from the stables, saying he had to take care of his brother who was drunk and delirious. Amos went upstairs and found William in bed, unwell, but neither drunk nor delirious. Charles, probably the worse for alcohol, came into the room, and tried to knock William about.

*West Street, Faversham, showing the Sun Inn and no. 12 next door – to the right of the picture. (Author's collection)*

When Amos went to protect the invalid, Charles made the mistake of grabbing the coachman and threatening to murder him. Amos, the more powerful man, threw Charles onto the bed, and then knocked him down. When Charles scrambled up and tried to get at his brother again, the coachman intervened once more, and there was a scuffle. Eventually Charles gave up the unequal struggle.

On another occasion when Amos and William returned from a journey, Charles angrily accused the doctor of bringing spirits into the house. When William protested that he had not, Charles attacked him. Amos was obliged to get between the brothers to protect the doctor from injury. Some time later, Amos heard a huge row going on in William's bedroom, and hurrying upstairs he found William lying unconscious on the floor. He picked the doctor up and put him on the bed. Charles was in a drunken rage, and accused his brother of having whisky in the house. Determined to find it, he started searching frantically through everything in the room. The drawers were locked, and Charles demanded that William, who had recovered consciousness, give him the keys. William had enough presence of mind to hand them to Amos, but Charles, refusing to be thwarted, got a chisel and began prising the drawers open. He was able to open all of them except for the small one in which William kept the treasured mementoes of his dead wife. Charles went and got a bigger chisel and broke open that drawer too, pulling out the contents; lace, crape, and other things, and throwing them all over the room. Throughout this desperate performance, William was very distressed, crying and begging Charles not to do it. 'Oh, b****r your wife,' was Charles' reply. William remained in bed and Amos stayed by him. Between 10 and 11 o'clock that night Charles returned to the room, and began throwing about everything that was moveable, including glass bottles and the toilet set (some of which hit William) and as he did so, threatened repeatedly to murder his brother. Mrs Lyddon looked in from time to time and threw boots at the doctor. The disturbance lasted until 2 a.m. William remained in bed for two days and two nights, and Amos stayed with him the whole time. The coachman later stated that he had not dared to close his eyes in sleep, although it seems unlikely that he didn't doze at least part of the time.

On the second night a bottle and a glass appeared by the doctor's bedside. Neither William nor Amos had brought them in or seen who had. Amos was unable to read, but saw that the bottle had a red label on it and suspected it was poison. The doctor took up the glass and was about to drink from it when Amos struck it out of his hand. Amos showed the bottle to William, who said, 'That is poison; it must be', then threw his arms round Amos' neck saying, 'God bless you Amos'. When Charles came into the room Amos drew his attention to the bottle of poison and asked how it had come there, but Charles simply laughed. At the first opportunity, Amos disposed of the bottle. William later told Amos he was afraid to drink anything as he thought they meant to poison him.

Amos had been with the practice since 1886, but by 28 September 1889 he had had enough of the drunkenness and fights, and left. He was replaced by Harry Lyons, who also witnessed violent quarrels during which Charles and Mrs Lyddon struck William. He too had sometimes to intervene to prevent William from being injured. William was often locked out of the house and had to go and sit in the carriage until he was allowed back in. It was rare for William to retaliate. He appeared to be a crushed man, unable to defend himself, and only occasionally uttered a pathetic threat to hurt Charles in return. One night Inspector Fowle of the Faversham police, found Charles wandering drunkenly in the market place at midnight, and Charles told him he was afraid to go home because of his brother.

In March 1890 Charles went back to Gibson, complaining that his brother was collecting debts and not attending properly to the practice, thus wasting the estate. He wanted Gibson to take possession of the property on his behalf but Gibson declined to take such a serious step. In June, Charles complained to Gibson again and Gibson wrote to William saying that he was behaving improperly under the terms of the deed. There was no reply. From then on, Charles regularly called Inspector Fowle to the house to settle disturbances. When Fowle arrived, Charles would show him the keys to the house, and say that under the deed, he was master.

Although William denied having drink in his possession, he had for some time been prevailing upon the servants to bring in supplies, hiding both his drink and money from Charles. It is also possible that William had been helping himself to the drug supplies in the dispensary, although the extent to which he did this was never established.

On 4 August 1890 Charles Naylor, a fifteen-year-old page boy, was taken on by the practice, and was, during the ensuing months, the only person resident in the household who was neither a Lyddon nor a drunkard. Naylor's duties were to

*Inspector Fowle and his sons. (Courtesy of Kent Police Museum)*

look after the surgery, answer the door, help Mrs Lyddon with the cooking, and run errands, but he was also expected to learn dispensing. Charles gave Naylor strict instructions not to carry out any orders of William's, and in particular he did not want Naylor to bring the doctor supplies of alcohol. Despite this, Naylor often brought William quarts of beer and half pints of whisky.

On 27 September Inspector Fowle was called to West Street, where William told him, 'My brother is threatening me with a gun, and I cannot get into the surgery to do my business.' Fowle found Charles sitting in the dining room with a double barrelled gun saying, 'Yes, and if you come near me I'll use it.' Fowle calmly told him to put the gun away and never to use threats with a gun again or he would get into serious trouble. Even through his usual haze of drink, Charles realised he might have gone too far. He showed Fowle that the gun was not loaded, and laughed, saying he only did it to frighten William. Fowle did not find it funny and was issuing a stern warning when William entered the room. Charles punched his brother in the stomach, saying, 'Your breath stinks and I don't want it in my mouth.' William simply turned around without a word and went into the surgery. Fowle persuaded Charles to put the gun away.

Three days later, William Reed Hill, a Colchester doctor who had been visiting the Lyddons as a friend, became concerned about William's health and urged that a practitioner should be summoned. Charles sent a note to Dr J. Irvine Boswell asking him to come and see his brother, who was ill with pneumonia and pleurisy. When Boswell arrived later that evening he was told (presumably by Naylor) that Charles was not in a fit state to see him. Boswell insisted on seeing Charles and, on being conducted upstairs, he was appalled to find Charles lying on the landing, speechlessly drunk, together with a young woman in the same condition. William was in his bedroom very ill, dirty and neglected. Naylor told Boswell that William had had only a cup of tea and a glass of beer all day. The drunken young woman was his nurse. Boswell discussed the case with Hill and said that it would be fatal to allow William to remain. Hill agreed and said that he had been supplying William with food from his own house, as the patient had not been getting sufficient at home. The doctors arranged to remove William to the Faversham Cottage Hospital, where he remained for a week in a delirious state. When William came to his senses he told Boswell that he was distressed about the deed of assignment. On 26 October William left hospital against the advice of his doctor and also against his own inclinations. He told Boswell he had had letters from Charles and if he did not go home he would 'have to suffer more in the end as Charles stuck at nothing.'

There were no serious disturbances for the next three weeks, then on Wednesday 19 November Naylor overheard Charles accuse William of taking drugs. The following morning Charles told Mrs Lyddon that William had turned two patients out of the surgery and he could not have him in the house any more as he was ruining the practice. Charles telegraphed a solicitor, Mr John J. Wiggins of Whitstable, saying that William had been receiving money belonging to the practice for which he had not accounted, and it was essential that steps should be taken to establish the rights under the deed of assignment. Wiggins arrived and advised William to appoint a solicitor to assist him, but when William told Naylor to go and fetch a solicitor to act for him, Naylor refused, saying that Charles had forbidden him to do anything William asked him to do.

William was considerably the worse for drink, and Charles told him that if he did not go to a lodging house in Herne Bay to recuperate he would have to get out of the house. The trap was got ready and William drove to the railway station and travelled up to Herne Bay with Mrs Lyddon. There he was seen by a doctor, Charles Bowes, but refused to be examined although he was obviously very ill. That evening William tried to go out for a walk and was seen reeling about in the street,

*Faversham Cottage Hospital. (Author's collection)*

and eventually, after suffering a heavy fall, he had to be helped back to his lodgings. He spent a restless night during which he fell out of bed. He remained very ill on the following day but on Saturday he was improved, and by Sunday he was able to eat bread and milk. Charles came to collect him on Monday 24 November, when William was still too ill to walk unaided.

Wiggins wrote to Charles proposing a scheme under which the brothers could settle their differences, but events were soon to overtake this attempt at reconciliation.

William returned from Herne Bay just after midday. He seemed to be in better health and at 1.30 p.m. he ate some raw minced beef washed down with stout. Between 4 and 5 p.m. he went out in his trap to see some patients, and returned between 6 and 7 p.m. William then put up some medicines and Naylor took them out, returning between 9 and 10 p.m. That evening William saw a patient in his surgery at 9 p.m. and seemed to be sober and in fair health. His work done, it is probable that William turned to the comfort of drink. Later that evening he fell asleep on the couch in Mrs Lyddon's bedroom

When Charles saw this he told Naylor to go to the police station and fetch Inspector Fowle, as he wanted William turned out of the house. Fowle arrived at about 11.30 p.m. When Charles spoke to the inspector in the dining room it was obvious to Fowle that Charles was drunk. Charles said, 'You know all about it, the deed of assignment', and said that he wanted Lyddon to leave the house. Fowle asked where Lyddon was and Charles said he was upstairs lying on the couch, to which Fowle replied that Charles had best go to bed himself. Charles insisted on his brother leaving but Fowle pointed out that it was very cold outside and he would not agree to turn William out of doors. As he turned to leave, Charles followed him, insisting that he go upstairs and turn Lyddon out of the house. Mrs Lyddon met them in the hall. 'Yours is very kind advice, Sir,' she said to Fowle, 'and I am ashamed of Mr Lyddon to want to turn the doctor out as he is lying very ill and not fit to be turned out.' Lyddon again insisted saying that his solicitor, Mr Wiggins, had said his brother must leave the house. 'You are not bound to do what Mr Wiggins tells you,' said Fowle. Charles replied, 'My brother takes drugs and I might be accused of something.' Fowle, who must by then have been thoroughly fed up with being repeatedly called out to deal with disturbances at the Lyddons', left.

Charles and Mrs Lyddon then went upstairs. Naylor turned off the gas and when he went up there was another row going on, with Charles trying to hit William in the face and the doctor calling his brother a blackguard. Charles was accusing William of taking drugs, and Mrs Lyddon, hitting William on the shoulder several times with her fists, said, 'You had better take a damned good dose and then you would be out of the way.' Mrs Lyddon then picked up a wooden bonnet stand, saying she would crack his head open with it. Even Charles thought this was extreme and stopped her. Mrs Lyddon said William wanted horsewhipping to keep him from taking drugs, and Charles, who seemed to think this was a good idea, told Naylor to get the tandem whip, but the boy declined.

William went into his own bedroom, saying, 'the b******s will not let me alone.' Charles followed his brother and insisted that William should sleep in the small lumber room adjoining Mrs Lyddon's bedroom, but William refused, understandably as there was no bed in there. Naylor, who later described William as 'right down drunk', spoke to him, saying he thought he ought to go into the little room for the sake of peace and quiet. Reluctantly, William agreed. The bedclothes were taken from the doctor's bed and put in the lumber room. There was no means of lighting in the room so Naylor put a candle in there, but Charles made him remove it. It was shortly after midnight when William entered the small, dark, cold room, and Charles locked the door from the outside. Naylor usually shared a bedroom with Dr Lyddon but Charles said he had better stay with him that night. Charles remained almost fully clothed and it seems that the two shared a bed. Naylor slept soundly through the night.

The next morning, at about a quarter to eight, Charles woke Naylor and told him to get on with his work. Naylor went downstairs while Charles checked on William, and it was not until two hours later that Naylor went to look in on the doctor. William, who was fully dressed apart from his jacket and waistcoat, and covered only by a blanket, was apparently asleep but making a rattling noise in his throat. He was lying on a white sheet which was all there was between him and the floor. Charles and his mother came into the room and told Naylor to get William into Mrs Lyddon's room and put him on the bed. Neither offered to give the boy any assistance in moving what was essentially a dead weight. Naylor struggled for about fifteen minutes, pushing William along the floor feet first, along the corridor and down some steps, and finally getting him into Mrs Lyddon's room. There, he tried but failed to lift William onto the bed. Mrs Lyddon offered to help but Charles said that his brother should be left there. The doctor ended up sitting on the floor leaning against the bedstead.

Naylor thought William had stopped breathing, and Charles told him to go to Dr Evers of nearby Albion Terrace, and tell him to come and see Dr Lyddon as he was seriously ill. Naylor hurried to Dr Evers, who agreed to come in a while, but as soon as he returned Charles told him to go back to Evers and ask him to come at once because he thought his brother was dead. Meanwhile Charles had asked a neighbour, Mr Woodruff, to summon Dr Boswell saying he thought William was dead or dying. Evers and Boswell arrived within a few minutes of each other. William had slipped down to the floor and was lying face down, half under the bed. When he was turned over it was seen that his face was livid and congested. He was obviously quite dead.

Charles immediately asked for a death certificate, saying, 'you have been attending him Dr Boswell, and you know the cause of death.' Boswell replied that he did not know the cause of death and would certainly not give a certificate. Evers agreed with Boswell, and Charles, knowing that without a certificate he was obliged to contact the police, told Naylor to fetch Inspector Fowle. The first policeman to arrive at the scene was Sergeant Frederick Sargent, who arrived shortly after 11 a.m., and was told by Charles that his brother had slept in the lumber room because he was ill 'and wanted to go in there.' Sargent examined the body. Nearby he saw an 8oz medicine bottle tightly corked, lying on its side. He asked Charles if he could account for it. Charles took the bottle and said, 'this settles the mater: it is morphia. I am glad you have found this.' He handed the bottle to Sargent. 'I am glad you found this,' Charles repeated, 'or people might say that I poisoned him.' Charles then made an affecting display of grief over the fate of his 'poor brother'. Sargent later questioned Naylor, asking if he had seen the doctor with a bottle like that on the previous day. Naylor said he had not. 'Did he have a bottle like this when he went into the little room last night?' asked Sargent. 'No,' said Naylor, 'or I should have seen it,' although he admitted it might have been in a pocket.

Later that morning in the dispensary, Charles showed a morphia bottle to Naylor and said he thought William had been taking some of the contents. The last time Naylor had seen the bottle there was about 4oz in it, and that morning there was only about two.

When Fowle arrived he went up to see the body of Dr Lyddon and looked around for a suicide note, but found nothing. He saw that there was only one door into the lumber room which had a key on the bunch held by Charles Lyddon. There was no communication between the small room and Mrs Lyddon's room. It followed that no one could have gone into the lumber room during the night except Charles, who had charge of the only key, and he said he had not been in to see William until morning. Mrs Lyddon, however, told Naylor that she had first been into the lumber room to see William at 3 a.m. and had then gone to and fro to see him as his breath was so bad, after which she had called Charles to come and look at his brother. According to Mrs Lyddon, Charles had let her into the room.

The post-mortem examination was carried out by Drs Boswell and Evers and an assistant that same evening. They found bruises in the right side of the face, the shoulder and both sides of the trunk, but there were no life-threatening injuries. The lungs showed signs of William's recent illness. The liver, kidneys and stomach were all affected by alcohol abuse. Initial tests of fluid drawn from the stomach suggested that William had ingested a fatal dose of morphia. Boswell tied the ends of the stomach and placed it with a piece of the liver in a jar which he handed to Inspector Fowle.

The inquest opened on Wednesday 26 November and took place at the Guildhall, Faversham. It was presided over by Mr W.J. Harris, coroner for the district, and Mr Wiggins appeared on behalf of the Lyddons. Naylor was very hesitant about giving his crucial evidence, and was several times rebuked by the coroner who demanded to know if anyone had been talking to him and telling him what to say. Naylor revealed that when he had told the court how Mrs Lyddon had offered to strike Dr Lyddon with the bonnet stand, Wiggins had held up his hand and said 'Hush'. The inquest was adjourned.

On 27 November home office analyst Thomas Stevenson began his examination of the samples. He saw that the stomach and liver showed chronic degeneration due to alcohol, and the stomach fluids contained a fatal dose of morphine. Death would have taken place two to six hours after the dose was taken. This timing was crucial since it showed that the dose must have been taken during the night while William was occupying the lumber room.

On Saturday 29 November William Reeks Lyddon was buried at the parish church, Faversham. A crowd estimated at about 1,000 gathered for the event, and chiefly consisted of working people, amongst whom he had had many patients, and by whom he was greatly respected. Many tradesmen were also present and most of the shops in West Street and some in Court Street had closed shutters as a mark of respect. The cortège started from the house at 11 a.m. Hundreds of people lined the streets and followed the procession to the church. After the interment there were signs of a hostile demonstration towards Mrs Lyddon and Charles, who were guarded by four constables. The crowd hooted and a snowball was thrown. The Lyddons were quickly escorted to their carriage which sped off at a brisk pace, followed by hooting crowds.

At the resumed inquest on 9 December, Dr Boswell testified that if William had received medical attention within an hour of taking the morphia his life could have been saved. He had only ever known William take the drug in small medicinal quantities to treat the pain of his pleurisy. Once again as the enquiry was adjourned Charles needed a police guard to protect him from hostile crowds. Having come partly down the steps of the Town Hall he saw the people outside and retreated back indoors, not emerging until the crowds had dispersed. When the enquiry continued on 11 December he did not attend. Naylor was questioned very closely about the bottle found in the room with William, and said he was sure that he had seen no bottle in the doctor's possession when he had entered the room.

*Faversham Guildhall. (Author's collection)*

On the following morning when he helped William from the room there was no bottle in the position as described by the policeman. If it had been there he did not think he could have missed seeing it. He had never known William to take morphia or carry it with him. Amos then gave evidence of the shocking scenes of violence in the Lyddon household. He believed that the rows, which had only begun after the deed was signed, were started by Charles. William had once told him he had taken an oath never to strike Charles or Mrs Lyddon.

In the meantime, letters of administration had been granted on William's estate, and Mr Wiggins placed an advertisement in the newspapers asking for all the claimants to get in touch with him before 14 February, when he would make a distribution of the assets.

The inquest continued on 15 December and once again Charles did not attend. Naylor admitted that while he had been ordered not to bring drink to the doctor by Charles, he had in fact done so. William had given him money to take care of before he went into hospital because he said Charles took money from his pocket. Naylor had used the money to buy whisky in half pints from the Ship, but he had also bought it on the doctor's credit from The Sun, the Railway Hotel and the Royal William. He had never known William take drugs apart from in medicinal amounts. He thought the brothers were on good terms when they were both sober. In contradiction of Charles' claim, Naylor was adamant that William had not wanted to go into the lumber room to sleep.

*The Faversham Mystery. (Author's collection)*

When the inquest reconvened two days later Charles arrived in a cab and as soon as the crowd recognised him he was greeted with deep groans, which continued until he disappeared into the building. The hearing commenced with the local bank manager telling the court that the sum of £5,000 mentioned by Charles to Amos did not exist. Then came what the crowds had been waiting for, as Charles Lyddon gave evidence. He did so very clearly and with a confident air, asserting that William had been addicted to drugs and he had remonstrated with his brother about this many times. The quarrelling and fighting was, he said, all instigated by William. He claimed that William had been willing to go into the small room to sleep, where it was perfectly warm and comfortable. He added that he had checked on William several times on the morning of 25 November and had found him asleep and snoring. He denied all knowledge of the poison bottle. Asked what he had said to Naylor to get him to hurry up and fetch a doctor he declined to give the precise words with a laugh, and earned a stern reprimand from the coroner. 'This is no laughing matter. I am surprised that you should show such levity here.' Charles admitted that he had threatened his brother but said he only did it 'in chaff'. He was adamant that the door of the little room had been locked all night and said he had not unlocked it to admit Mrs Lyddon, but had stayed in bed all night. The inquest was adjourned for the last time and Charles walked back to the house in West Street accompanied by Inspector Fowle, Sergeant Sargent, and several constables while a large crowd followed, hooting vehemently. On the following day the jury went to the Lyddons' house accompanied by the police and made an inspection, particularly of the lumber room and the place where the poison bottle had been found.

The inquest re-convened on 19 December, when Sarah Wise, who had laid out the body of the deceased, said that Mrs Lyddon had told her she had gone into the lumber room three times during the night before William's death and found him in a deep sleep. Mrs Lyddon had said that on the third occasion, she had called Charles because William 'had got an awful countenance.' Despite two witnesses saying that Mrs Lyddon had told them she had been in the room, the lady herself was not called to give evidence.

The coroner summed up. He said that there was no doubt that William had died of poisoning with morphia. The deed of assignment was only of value to Charles if William died. Charles was unqualified and could not have carried on the practice if his brother lived, but if William died Charles had a valuable asset to sell. Due to William's habits the value of the practice was decreasing as was Charles' security. It was a remarkable fact that the little bottle of morphia did not appear upon the scene until after Charles found that he could not get a death certificate and there would have to be an inquest. The coroner added that if a person placed poison within reach of another who took it and died, the person placing it was guilty of the death. As to the differences between Charles' and Naylor's testimony, the jurymen must make up their own minds. After three quarters of an hour's deliberation, the jury found that morphia was 'feloniously administered to the deceased by Charles Lyddon.' Charles was taken into custody, to the great delight of the crowds who waited outside.

Without his daily supply of whisky Charles was in some difficulties. At 2 a.m. the next morning he was seized with a violent fit and a doctor was called out to him. In contrast with his previous confident air, he presented a somewhat woebegone appearance at the magistrates' hearing, which took place at the Guildhall on 20 and 23 December. It was reported by the *Faversham Mercury* that Mrs Lyddon had left Faversham 'for a few days' change' and within days, the furniture and effects of no. 12 West Street were advertised for sale. The auction took place on 8 January and attracted a huge number of people who crowded into the house eager for a look at the room in which William Lyddon had died. They were to be disappointed, since the door was firmly shut and almost hidden by the furniture stacked against it.

*Scenes from The Faversham Mystery. (Author's collection)*

When the police court hearings took place at the Guildhall in January, the market place was thronged with spectators. Charles, who was then lodged in St Augustine's Prison, Canterbury, was brought to Faversham under strict police surveillance to be formally charged with murder. He was obliged to travel by the early train to avoid public demonstrations of hostility. Charles had not shaved for some weeks, and presented a very dejected air. He sat in court between Superintendent Mayne and Inspector Fowle, arms folded, legs crossed, his head bent and eyes either closed or their gaze fixed upon the ground. Once again, Mrs Lyddon was not called to give evidence. At the hearing on 22 January, Mr Wiggins was unexpectedly absent, his place taken by a Mr Mercer, and when Charles was committed for trial at the Kent winter assizes at Maidstone on 16 February, Wiggins, who should have been brought as a witness, did not attend.

The trial was transferred to the Old Bailey, and opened on 18 March 1891. The defence was handled by Henry Fielding Dickens, son of Charles Dickens. Mr Wiggins could not be called as a witness as in the interim he had absconded with £300 of Charles' money.

Mr Murphy QC for the prosecution commented in his opening speech on the prisoner's financial motives for committing murder, Charles' failure to call medical assistance when it must have been clear to him early on the morning of 25 November that his brother was dangerously ill, and the fact that William's life could have been saved by prompt action. The only person who had the key to the room, and who could have supplied the deadly drug, was Charles.

Mr Dickens addressed the court with supreme confidence. He said that the case against the prisoner had completely broken down, and stated as a fact that William had been hopelessly addicted to morphia. Ignoring the substantial evidence of hysterical scenes and violence in the Lyddon household, he claimed that the brothers had been mainly on amicable terms and any threats had been 'in chaff'.

There was no direct evidence of administration of poison by Charles, and the case against him was pure inference. The deed of assignment had been amicable and Charles had not appropriated the practice income for himself but had used it to pay business debts. Dickens submitted that William had taken the morphine bottle into the lumber room in his coat pocket, which explained why Naylor had not seen it, and had himself taken the dose which caused his death. Mr Justice Hawkins in summing up emphasised to the jury that if there was any reasonable doubt they must return a verdict of not guilty, and they almost immediately did so. Charles was a free man, and a fortunate one, since had he been tried in Kent shortly after being committed, the strength of public feeling might well have resulted in a different verdict.

The national newspapers concurred with the result. The *Daily Chronicle* made the point that Charles had made determined efforts to stop William getting whisky, and suggested that, unable to get his supplies, William had turned to morphia. *The Globe* commented in a dry understatement, 'Indeed, taking the evidence as a whole, the Lyddon household was not one of those well-regulated families in which accidents are unlikely to happen.' The death of William Reeks Lyddon remains an unsolved mystery.

Charles and his mother did not return to no. 12 West Street but went to lodge at no. 1 Marina, Herne Bay, the same boarding house where William had stayed in the previous year. Charles was both the administrator and assignee of the estate, and in June 1891 he issued 168 summonses against William's patients in an attempt to recover £600 of debts, in many cases obtaining judgement for the full amount. He probably spent the rest of his short life spending his brother's money on drink. Charles Lyddon died of bronchitis and exhaustion in a Southwark lodging-house in 1895, aged thirty-three. His estate was worth just £14.

# 9

# A TRAGEDY OF RECKLESS FOLLY

*Whitstable, 1926*

Alfonso Francis Austin Smith (usually known as 'Frank') was born in Toronto in 1889. His grandfather was wealthy businessman Sir Frank Smith, and young Frank was assured of a life of ease and privilege. He was sent to England at the age of ten, and was educated at a private school and later Cambridge University. In 1909 he joined the 4th Dragoon Guards. Mixing in high society, he squandered much of his fortune on extravagant living. He made heavy losses gambling on horses and at cards, and later fell into the hands of unscrupulous money lenders. In October 1912 he married Ruth Bernadette Wynne, the American-born daughter of Robert John Wynne, a telegrapher who had risen to be postmaster general and later US Consul. The honeymoon was hardly over before the young couple realised they had made a mistake. In the following year they agreed to separate. In 1919 Smith met petite, pretty Rosina Ivy Wight, usually known as 'Kathleen', who was eleven years his junior. They fell in love and were soon living together. In 1922 Smith obtained a divorce from Ruth, and in May 1925 he and Kathleen were married. By this time the couple had a son and two daughters.

In December 1925 the Smiths were living in Herne Bay when they met John Derham. John Adam Tytler Derham, born in 1886, was the eldest son of a barrister, Walter Derham, and grandson of John Adam Tytler VC. Derham was educated at Eton and Cambridge University. In 1913 he married Consuelo de Colegan, at Blean, and there were three children of the marriage, but by 1925 he and his wife were living apart. A lanky athletic figure, he was for many years captain of the Herne Bay rink hockey team, and had represented England in international matches. Frank Smith and Derham became friends and soon Derham was a frequent visitor to the Smiths' home.

Over the next few months the Smiths' marriage slowly fell apart. Smith suspected that his wife and Derham were having an affair, and he sought consolation in heavy drinking. There were rows between the men, and on one occasion after Derham told Smith he thought Kathleen was in love with him, Smith challenged him to a duel. They fought with fists instead, and while Derham was a powerful man, Smith had learned some fighting skills, and was able to knock Derham to the floor. As Derham shakily got to his feet Smith delivered a knockout punch. When his rival came round, Smith fetched water and told Derham to bathe his face, and get out. Smith hoped that this would end the affair, but in June 1926, he went to London on business, and learned that while he was away, Kathleen and Derham had continued to see each other.

Kathleen had decided that her marriage was over, and asked her solicitors to prepare a deed of separation and send it to her husband for his approval. Smith knew nothing of her intentions until the document arrived. Although the couple were now living apart he hoped it was only a temporary separation. He was drinking even more heavily than usual, although it brought him little solace, and wrote letters to Derham both abusing and threatening him.

On 10 July Derham went to stay at his mother's house in Gladstone Park Gardens, Cricklewood, while Kathleen went to live at Derham's home, Claverhouse, in Herne Bay. Incensed with drink-fuelled jealousy, Smith determined to gather evidence of adultery. On 14 July he went to the Cricklewood house in Derham's absence, where he found and removed two photographs of his wife from the sitting room. He then

*Picture from* The People – *Mrs Smith. (Author's collection)*

wrote a letter to Derham's mother who was very ill in hospital. He must have been in a desperate frame of mind to write to a sick woman in these terms:

> No doubt you are aware that your son Jack has seduced my wife. She is somewhere with him now and confesses to the attractions he holds. I have sufficient proof for my solicitors, but the satisfaction I will obtain with my own hands.

On the following day Smith went to Claverhouse, where a nanny, Miss Wyatt, was looking after the children. Asking for his wife, he was told she was not in, and went up to her room and removed a letter. He seemed quite calm at the time, and took the children out, but when he returned that afternoon it was obvious that he had been drinking. He told Miss Wyatt to take the children to their grandfather in London because he was going to smash up the house. 'Do you think I am going to let another man take my wife?' he exclaimed. 'I will do for you first: I will kill them both. I don't care if I am arrested.' In his rage, he started tearing pictures from the walls. Miss Wyatt fled upstairs with the children, and for a quarter of an hour afterwards heard the sound of things smashing.

On the following day Smith wrote to Derham:

> You damned swine. I only wish you had the courage to meet me. You have seduced my wife, and for that you think you will get off easily in the Divorce Court. You took my wife. I have taken something from you. Go and find out what. You dirty white-livered fool. You lied to me and now you are going to suffer. If you are any sort of a man you will meet me face to face. You must realize you have ruined not only a very sweet girl, but the woman I and not you, love. If you really loved her you could not have done it.

Smith called on his wife's solicitors where he showed the managing clerk Frederick Barwood the letters he had found written by Derham to Kathleen and asked if they gave him grounds for a divorce. Barwood declined to give any advice at that point and Smith left in a highly agitated state, saying he would find Derham and 'smash him up.'

On 26 July Kathleen took a house in St Anne's Road, Tankerton, Whitstable, called 'Stella Maris', and four days later, her sixteen-year-old sister Lillian came to stay, bringing the three children.

Smith had not given up on repairing the marriage. He wrote a long letter to Kathleen on 2 August expressing his love for her, promising that he would make a home for her and the children and give up drinking:

> My heart is absolutely broken and I tell you that I cannot go on living without you. I will deal with that damn cad Derham first ... I cannot live without you, nor do I intend to. For the children's sake, send him away. If ever I can find him again, I will deal with him whatever it may lead to ...

In the last paragraph, referring to his son, he made his thoughts very clear, 'Jackie won't want to have fingers pointed at him as the son of a murderer of an unfaithful wife and her lover, and a suicide. Come back to me, my girl, my little white heather.'

Smith arranged an appointment to meet his wife at the Grosvenor Hotel on Friday 6 August to discuss the position, but she did not turn up. Frantically he wrote, 'If I do not hear from you on Monday I will do something really desperate', to which he added, 'God help Derham if he is coming to Tankerton. I have not started on him yet.'

Three days later he wired her and she responded. It was agreed that he would go down to Stella Maris to see her. On the same day Smith borrowed a Webley service revolver, and some cartridges from a friend, David Harrower, on the pretext that he was going to Ireland and wanted it for protection against the Sinn Feiners. That evening he arrived at Stella Maris, and he and Kathleen talked. Discussing his thoughts of suicide, he showed her the gun. If she had not taken his threats seriously before she certainly did so then, and she tried to placate him, saying that she would think over the situation and they would talk about it again the next day. That night Kathleen slept in the spare room while her husband took the bedroom. On the following day Kathleen told Lillian that her husband had a gun hidden in the house. They searched, and Lillian found the heavy revolver in the coal box. She took it out and hid it in the glove box in the hall. The next day Smith and his wife talked again, and, still afraid of what he might do, she told him what he wanted to hear, that she would end the relationship with Derham. The couple slept in the same bedroom that night, and also on the next. All seemed well and on 11 August Smith wrote a note to his wife expressing his happiness at the resolution of their problems:

> My own adorable little wife. You have made me happier than ever I hoped to be. I have been mad lately and in hell. Now you have given me glimpses of the heaven which, with your help, my wife, I leave no stone unturned to reach.

He begged her forgiveness for 'two reckless and foolish things' he had done – possibly the visits to gather evidence – and expressed his desire to bury the past. 'I feel like a man who has been in a terrible fever, delirious and wandering, and am just waking from a deep, refreshing, and life-giving sleep.'

On the same day, however, he discovered that Kathleen had been continuing to receive letters from Derham, collecting them from the post office. Intercepting a letter addressed to Kathleen, he found it was a love-letter from Derham. He realised then that she had been lying to him, and that the affair with Derham was far from over. He returned to Stella Maris to confront her.

They talked again and he pleaded with her, but this time to no purpose, and Kathleen suggested that he should leave. He wrote another note:

My dear, dear girl, this problem can only be solved in one way, the removal of your lover Derham or myself ... The whole thing is too mean and too disgusting for me. I can't stand still while I live and go on supporting this great agony of mind and heart. May God forgive me for what I am about to do, and may he forgive you, the cause of it all. As to your lover, you will always have this between you, and if you can go on after it there are no sentences in the language which could be construed to express what you both are ... My heart is broken and there is nothing in life for me.

Lillian remained uneasy about the presence of the revolver in the house. On 12 August she went to check on it. It had gone. That day, John Derham received a telegram. It read:

Will you come down for a few hours tonight. Urgent. Wire K.I. Smith, G.P.O., Whitstable, not house. Come house if I am not at station. KATHLEEN.

Derham arrived at Stella Maris on the evening of 12 August. He had been trying to avoid meeting Smith, and was alarmed to be greeted by him at the door. Calmly, Smith said that it was he who had sent the telegram, and he just wanted to talk. Much against his inclinations, Derham went in, and the three sat down to discuss the situation. Kathleen made no effort to hide the affair, saying she wanted to be with Derham. Smith suggested that he and Derham should both go away and not see her for three months to give them all some time to think, but Derham and Kathleen retorted that it was he who should go away, suggesting Paris, where a cheap divorce could be had. Smith suddenly produced the revolver from his pocket and said he would settle everything by shooting himself. There was a struggle, and Derham took the gun from Smith and handed it to Kathleen who left the room. Lillian had been outside listening to the discussion. Kathleen handed her the gun and she hid it in the garden.

Kathleen was anxious to remove the cartridges, so later that evening, she asked Lillian for the gun, and tried to open it but was unable to do so. In desperation she took it into the kitchen, and held it under a running tap in an attempt to put it out of action. Smith came in and saw what was happening. 'Give it to me. I want to sell it,' he said. As Derham entered the kitchen, Smith took the gun from his wife and opened it, the cartridges falling out onto the table. Lillian snatched some of them but Smith put the others, and the gun, into his pocket. Shortly afterwards, Derham, Smith and his wife left the house and went to the Marine Hotel, where they had supper and talked things over, while Lillian went to bed. Just before 11 p.m. everyone was back at Stella Maris. Smith wanted his rival to leave the house, but Kathleen asked Lillian to help prepare a bed in the spare room for Derham. While they were doing this, Smith, who was getting increasingly agitated, came up to his wife several times. 'I won't have this other lover of yours sleeping in the house,' he said, but she only laughed. Shortly afterwards Lillian returned to her bedroom and the others went down to the drawing room, where Kathleen and

Derham began to sort cards in preparation for a game of bridge. Smith told them he did not want to play cards and intended to kill himself. The others reacted with calm disbelief.

Not long afterwards James Browning Barton, a builder of Whitstable, who was walking along St Anne's Road was passing by Stella Maris, and saw Derham and Kathleen standing in the middle of the drawing-room. Derham's right arm was stretched out pointing away from Smith who was standing by the window. Walking on, Barton heard a shot fired from inside the house, and quickly turned to look. He saw Derham and Kathleen making a sudden dash for Smith, pushing him towards the window. Smith fell, and there was a crash of glass as the pane broke, then Smith appeared to have been pulled down to the floor. Barton saw Derham raise his arm and strike at the fallen man.

Lillian was in bed when she heard the bang, and came running downstairs to the drawing-room where she saw Smith lying on the floor, and Derham sitting across him striking him on the head and shoulders with the gun. Kathleen, crying out 'Don't, don't', was trying to drag Derham off her husband, begging him to hand the revolver to her. Lillian came to help her sister and eventually the two women succeeded in getting Derham to desist. Lillian, who must have assumed that the worst was then over, but that she might be needed later to help her sister, went upstairs and quickly got dressed.

Derham had risen to his feet. He held the revolver in both hands, and was pressing it to his stomach. He lurched into the passageway and as Lillian rushed downstairs again she saw him opening the front door. Staggering out of the house he reached the pavement where he collapsed. Lillian followed him, and her one thought was the revolver, which she took from his hand and hid in the bushes.

Barton immediately went for medical help, and soon returned accompanied by Dr Whitney, who examined Derham. At Smith's invitation he went into the house where he saw two other men, passers-by who had gone in to help. Smith, with his face covered in blood, was in an extremely agitated condition He was rambling in his speech and reeked of alcohol. He asked:

> Have I killed him? Derham has been carrying on with my wife and I had no option but to put him out. You three gentlemen will make a good jury, and I know will give an honest verdict. I love my wife dearly. She invited him here. One of us had to go.

He later added that he believed his wife to be innocent. He asked Barton how Derham was, and Barton replied that to the best of his belief Derham was only slightly injured. After a pause, Smith said, 'What a fool; what a fool.'

Dr Whitney's examination showed that the bullet had entered Derham's left side, more toward the back of the body than the front, and had entered the abdomen. The wound could not have been self-inflicted. He arranged to have the stricken man taken to St Helier's Nursing Home, and then went to look at Smith's injuries. There were cuts on Smith's forehead, and on the back of his head, but Whitney reassured him that there was not much wrong with him. 'I hope I have given the other fellow a better one,' said Smith.

The police were called and as he was being taken away Smith handed a sealed envelope to police sergeant Quested, saying, 'I have written a letter to my wife. You may as well have it now.' He then opened it, adding, 'You may as well read this letter, it will explain matters. My wife started talking about divorce proceedings. I would not listen to her. I intended to shoot myself, but in the struggle it went off and shot Derham.' When Smith was told by an inspector that he would be detained, he asked, 'How is he? Where is the seducer?' A doctor who examined Smith at the prison confirmed that Smith had been drinking, and found two cuts on his forehead, which could have been caused by being struck with the butt of the revolver. A search of Smith's possessions revealed the deed of separation, which was unsigned.

On 13 August Smith was remanded at Canterbury charged with attempted murder, but on the same day, Derham died from the effects of his wound.

On 3 September Smith appeared at Canterbury Police Court charged with murder. The director of public prosecutions was represented by Mr Arthur Sefton Cohen, and Smith by a Mr Kimber. Cohen explained to the court that if Smith's claim was true and the gun had gone off accidentally while he was trying to commit suicide (then a criminal offence), he had shot Derham while attempting to commit a felony and should therefore be committed for trial. There was however clear evidence which suggested that Smith was not telling the truth. There was no blackening or charring around the entry wound which might have been expected if it had been fired at close quarters during a struggle, and the direction of the shot was from behind and downwards.

Walter Derham, who was then living at Sellinge, appeared to give evidence, but all he could say was that he had had no knowledge of the friendship between his son and the Smiths. Derham must have been a figure of considerable sympathy, for his wife had died on 27 August.

Lillian testified that Smith and her sister quarrelled frequently but she thought that otherwise they were 'all right'. Asked about Smith's drinking habits she said she could not describe him as a sober man.

Kimber did his best for his client. He submitted that there were no grounds for a murder charge as there was no evidence that Smith had discharged a revolver, and the very highest charge possible was manslaughter. The court disagreed, and the magistrate Charles Hardy committed Smith for trial at the next assizes on a charge of murder. Asked if he had any comment to make, Smith said, 'I have nothing to say, except that I am not guilty.'

The inquest resumed at Whitstable on 28 September, presided over by the Sittingbourne coroner, Mr E.C. Harris. Smith was again represented by Mr Kimber and the Derham family had appointed Mr A.K. Mowll. Letters written by Smith to Derham were produced in evidence. One read:

*Police constable, c. 1930. (Courtesy of Kent Police Museum)*

You have endeavoured to, or have accomplished, stealing my wife. You stole my wife after eating my bread. I retaliate in other ways. I only wish you had the courage to meet me. You seduced my wife, and for that you think you will get off easily in the Divorce Court. You intrigue to bring about a separation for your own ends; in other words, you wrecked my home.

Sergeant Quested showed the court the letter handed to him by Smith, in which the writer stated that he could not go on supporting this 'great agony of mind and heart' and intended to take his own life.

The jury had no difficulty in deciding that Derham had died from the gunshot wound, but felt that there was not sufficient evidence to show by whom the shot was fired and whether by accident or design. They found an open verdict.

By the time the case came to trial at the Kent Assizes in Maidstone on 25 November there were two charges against Smith, murder and being in possession of a firearm with intent to endanger life. A charge of attempting to commit suicide was not proceeded with. The prosecution was led by Mr Roland Oliver KC. The case was tried before seventy-five-year-old Mr Justice Avory. Stern, austere, and emotionless, his mask-like face had earned him the soubriquet 'the Sphinx of the Courts' and his severe and relentless pursuit of justice had made him one of the most notorious 'hanging judges' of his time.

Pictures from The Illustrated Police News. (Author's collection)

*Mr Justice Avory.
(Author's collection)*

The defence was that the shot had been fired by accident during a struggle, but not only did the medical evidence suggest otherwise, there was the eye-witness account of Barton, who told the court that he had seen the men standing at some distance apart shortly before the shot was fired, and only closing up afterwards. Smith had only one thing in his favour; he had secured the services of Sir Edward Marshall Hall, KC, for the defence. Hall's courtroom style was best described by the Lord High Chancellor the Earl of Birkenhead:

> The élan with which he swept down upon a doubtful jury, brushing aside their prejudices, and persuading them against their will, sometimes possibly against their better judgement, into accepting his own sanguine view of his client's innocence, won many a day which a more timorous, if not less skilful, advocate must have given up for lost.

For Smith to have any chance at all he needed every ounce of Hall's formidable powers.

Both Smith's solicitor and Hall suggested to their client that he should plead guilty to manslaughter, in which case they were confident he would receive a sentence of no more than five years, of which he would only have to serve three years nine months. Hall and Oliver put the suggestion to Avory who rejected the idea, to Smith's relief, as he had already seen prison reduce men to 'soulless hopeless husks' while on remand.

Oliver was in some difficulty. As he explained to the court, when Derham had been shot, only two other people were in the room, Smith and his wife. Since it was not permitted in law to call the defendant's wife as a witness for the prosecution, he would not be able to call an eye-witness to the actual shooting.

Marshall Hall placed a glimmer of doubt in the minds of the jury when he asked David Harrower how Smith had placed the borrowed revolver in his pocket. Harrower said it had been in his hip pocket, the muzzle pointing upwards and was obliged to agree that if a man was trying to take it out of his pocket and another man tried to seize it, the first point he would take hold of was the barrel. Hall also managed to extract from the doctor a grudging admission that it was possible for the wound to have been caused in a struggle.

Sir Edward Marshall Hall, KC. (Author's collection)

The most damning evidence against Smith was that of Barton. 'I suggest,' said Hall, 'that the mental picture which you formed of what you saw was a little wrong in time, if only a matter of a fraction of a second. I suggest that those two people jumped towards the prisoner before the shot went off.' Mr Justice Avory felt this needed clarification, and asked, 'Were Derham and Mrs Smith moving towards the prisoner after the shot was fired?'

'They were still moving towards the prisoner, and they all had their hands up,' replied Barton, unshaken by Hall's question. 'The prisoner was moving backwards towards the window.'

The noted gunsmith Robert Churchill, a witness in many a notorious criminal case, and a personal friend of Marshall Hall, gave evidence, stating that the wound had not been made close-up.

Hall, a lover of the dramatic demonstration in court, took up the revolver and asked Churchill to help him re-enact the struggle and show how the wound might have been inflicted as Smith claimed. Hall was a large powerful man, and used considerable force to try and turn Churchill's wrist to try and show how the gun might have been twisted to cause Derham's wound. Churchill, who did not believe Smith's claim that the revolver was in his hip pocket, refused to play along, and Hall, finding that Churchill was too strong for him, was obliged to turn to the doctor and Mr Oliver for his demonstration.

Hall strongly advised Smith against giving evidence, as it was his belief that he stood a better chance of acquittal if he did not, but Smith insisted, feeling that he could engage the sympathy of the jury.

The second day of the trial was mainly taken up with Smith's evidence. As he stepped into the witness box with soldierly dignity, wearing a symbolic sprig of white heather in his buttonhole, the sympathetic glances of the spectators indicated that his confidence had not been misplaced. Marshall Hall made sure to read out the passionate letter written by Smith to his wife on 11 August. As Smith, with tears streaming down his face, acknowledged that it was an honest expression of his feelings that day, a woman juror collapsed in hysterics, and all around the court there was the sound of sobbing. The judge ordered an adjournment and the juror left the court, returning after five minutes. Speaking of the death of Derham, Smith said he went to unbutton the back pocket of his trousers to take out the revolver. He confirmed that he was standing with his back to the window but claimed that the curtains were drawn and no one could see into the room from outside unless peering through the crack. Smith said that all he was aware of was a struggle, a bang and being struck on the head. The next thing he could remember was speaking to Inspector Rivers. He swore that he had not pulled the trigger. Under cross-examination Smith maintained that he had never threatened or intended to harm Derham, but Oliver read out extracts from his letters which could have had no other interpretation. All Smith could say was, 'I was in such a state of mind that I did not know what I wrote or meant.'

In the note Smith had handed to Sergeant Quested, Smith had stated that he intended to shoot himself, but having received legal advice since then, he had changed his story. If he had meant to shoot himself, then in law he had formed the intention to kill, and the death of Derham, even if the gun had gone off by accident, was murder. Questioned by Mr Justice Avory, Smith said that when he pulled out the revolver his only intention had been to demonstrate that he had the means of shooting himself.

Avory asked a very pertinent question. 'Then I want to know this. In that state of affairs, how could you think that getting Derham to the house on the evening of the twelfth would assist in a reconciliation?' Weakly, Smith said he thought he could get Derham to see 'the folly of it all.'

'How could you suppose that the presence of Derham would assist in effecting reconciliation with your wife?' demanded Avory. Smith suggested that he might have appealed 'to his better nature.'

'After you called him a damned swine, could you really appeal to his better nature?' said Avory, dryly.

In his closing address Hall's main theme was to convince the jury that Smith had no intention of killing Derham, and though he had contemplated suicide, his hope up to the very last was for reconciliation. He ended with an impassioned appeal to the jury to give the prisoner the chance of resuming 'his old happy life with the woman he loves, which has been so long denied to him.' As ever, Hall's moving eloquence held the onlookers spellbound.

Mr Justice Avory clearly believed in Smith's guilt. In a stern summing up he referred pointedly to the fact that Mrs Smith had not been called as a witness for the defence. Was it conceivable that if she could support the prisoner's version of events that she would not have been called? He asked the jury to consider if there could be any possible explanation for her absence from the witness box except that she could not have supported her husband's story. In this case, he said, there were three possible verdicts. If they thought that Smith deliberately pulled the trigger with intent to kill either Derham or himself, he was guilty of murder. If he had no intention of shooting anyone but was simply removing the revolver from his pocket when it went off, he was entitled to be acquitted. There were a number of scenarios in which a verdict of manslaughter was appropriate – if he was provoked by an act of assault, was guilty of gross negligence in handling a firearm he knew to be loaded, if it had discharged by accident as he withdrew it to use it unlawfully, or, and this was the prisoner's story – he did not intend to shoot anyone but it discharged during a struggle for its possession.

Avory made it clear that he did not accept Smith's story. Why did Smith lure Derham to Whitstable with the telegram on the same day he obtained a revolver? Why, if he did not intend to use the gun did he dry the cartridges and reload it? If Smith did not intend to shoot anyone why was there a struggle for the gun? It would be difficult, urged Avory, for the jury to conclude it was a mere accidental shooting. Avory suggested that what Barton had seen was Derham sheltering Mrs Smith from harm with his right arm which caused his body to turn so he was struck in the left side by the bullet. If, as the gunsmith had said, the bullet must have been fired from at least 12 inches away was it likely that the revolver could have been fired in the way the prisoner stated?

The jury was out for over two hours during which time they asked to examine the revolver. On returning they found Smith not guilty of both murder and manslaughter. As Churchill was later to observe, 'Marshall Hall, against all the scientific evidence, carried the day again.' All around the court women could be heard sobbing with relief.

There was a shuffling of feet as spectators prepared to leave but Mr Justice Avory had not finished with Smith. He leaned forward to the clerk of the court. 'There is another charge on the calendar against the prisoner' he said quietly.

On the advice of Marshall Hall, Smith pleaded guilty to the second charge of being in possession of a firearm and cartridges with intent to endanger life. 'In view of the verdict of the jury' said Mr Justice Avory 'I assume that you had these in your possession with the intention of endangering the life of no other person than yourself. I must assume that. I have my own opinion upon it.' He sentenced Smith to an unusually severe term; twelve months with hard labour. Avory even managed to get a subtle revenge on the jury. After a murder trial it is usual for the judge to formally excuse the jury from further service for a substantial term, and the customary application was made. 'I see no reason why they should be so excused' said Avory.

In the light of the facts the jury's verdict is hard to fathom, but it may have been one of those cases when they voted with their emotions and not their heads. Smith, though unstable, was very much the injured party. His wife was having an affair and Derham was a married man. The jury had been warned that whatever his grievances, Smith was not entitled to take the law into his own hands, but somehow he had gained their sympathy, and for that he had to thank Marshall Hall.

The 'Stella Maris case', as it came to be known, was the last capital case in the career of Marshall Hall. He died after a short illness less than two months later, aged sixty-eight.

As Smith did his hard labour, articles about his life and marriages appeared in *The People* newspaper in November and December 1926, which Smith later denied he had written. The newspaper announced that he and Kathleen would be reunited but whether or not this happened is unknown, and if they were, the reconciliation did not last. It was not until Smith's release that his account of events was published in *The People* in October and November 1927. 'My whole life,' he wrote, 'has been a tragedy of reckless folly.' He continued to maintain that the death of Derham had been an accident. In March 1928, *Good Housekeeping* magazine published an article about capital punishment, which referred to the Stella Maris case and stated, 'the murdered man's wife expressed her personal relief at the acquittal of the man who had been tried.' The use of the expression 'murdered man' was somewhat unfortunate, and Smith brought an action for libel against the publishers which was heard in November and December 1928. He was then living at Riverside, Coombe Martin, Somerset, describing himself as a 'gentleman farmer'. He was awarded damages of £500. Despite this, times were hard financially. A receiving order had been made against him in 1921, but this was rescinded in 1928.

Later that year an unusual action was brought. Smith's divorce from his first wife, Ruth, had been granted in New York, and she had subsequently remarried. Since Smith did not have American domicile, the courts refused to accept the divorce, and it followed that the marriage to Kathleen was no marriage at all. A decree of nullity was brought by Kathleen who was by then living in Paris, and it was granted in November 1928.

In 1937 Smith was living in Walnut Tree Road, Heston, Middlesex, and was at law again, claiming damages from *Everybody's Weekly*, which had published an article in April that year. The article, claimed Smith, implied that he had only been acquitted because of the cleverness of his defending counsel. Smith cut a somewhat pathetic figure in court. He described himself as a freelance journalist. His two daughters were now nearly eighteen and sixteen and lived in France. His son Jackie was dead, having burned to death in a school fire. He had been bankrupt on four occasions, and in 1931 had been sentenced to six months in prison on a charge of obtaining £38 16s credit while an undischarged bankrupt. He had one very acute exchange. Mr Eddy for the defence asked Smith if he appreciated that the defendants unreservedly accepted that he was completely innocent and deserved the deepest sympathy. The Lord Chief Justice intervened; 'Do you know at what time they began to accept that?'

'At this very moment, I should say, my Lord,' replied Smith. Smith was awarded damages of £1,000.

In 1939 he sued the proprietors of the *Empire News*, which had published an article on the famous cases of Robert Churchill. He claimed that the article could be interpreted as suggesting that he was only acquitted because of the eloquence of counsel. This time the Lord Chief Justice ruled that the words were not capable of having a defamatory meaning. Smith took no further actions. He remarried in 1942 and died in 1944 aged 54.

# 10

# SHORE LEAVE

## *Gravesend, 1926*

Northfleet, near Gravesend, on the shores of the Thames with its ready supplies of water and timber, has long been a busy industrial area. In 1830 a new building scheme initiated by Joseph Rosher gave its name to Rosherville New Town, where gardens, only one of the attractions of the new and flourishing tourist trade, were laid out in 1837 for the entertainment of visitors arriving by steamboat from London. In the 1920s, United States naval vessels, on exercises in the Atlantic, moored in the Thames off Gravesend, and the men came ashore to Rosherville to enjoy the dance halls and social clubs. In 1926 the visiting flotilla included the USS *Sharkey* and the USS *Lardner*, both Clemson-class destroyers commissioned in 1919.

George Edwin Jenner, of no. 50 Gordon Road, Rosherville, was an employee of Imperial Paper Mills Ltd, which had its own wharf near Northfleet. At 11 p.m. on the night of Thursday 26 August 1926 he was returning home from work. Emerging from St Mark's Road where it joined London Road, he heard what he thought were four or five gunshots. As he turned left in the direction of home, four girls, a number of civilians, and some American sailors ran towards and then past him. One of the girls was heard to cry out, 'Who is that shooting?' Opposite 'The Larches' he saw a sailor lying in the road. The man was struggling to get to his feet, and Jenner went to help, but the man was in great pain and could only say that he had been shot. With the help of another passer-by, Jenner got the man onto a bus and took him to Gravesend Hospital, on Bath Street. They arrived at 11.10 p.m. where the wounded sailor was examined by the house surgeon, Dr Watt. Watt found a gunshot wound in the man's abdomen, and superficial abrasions on one knee. Blood loss was causing the patient to go into shock, but he was able to tell Watt that he was Emilio Paredes, a Filipino mess attendant on the USS *Sharkey*, and he had been shot by a man called Smith, who was gunner's mate on the USS *Lardner*. An operation was performed the following day, and on opening the abdomen the surgeon found five perforations of the small intestine, and one of the mesenteric arteries. He did not find any bullets.

USS *Lardner*. *(Author's collection)*

*The junction of London Road and Beresford Road, Gravesend, 2008. (Author's collection)*

The patient's case was declared hopeless, and Paredes, who was just twenty-three years old, was told that he was dying.

On the same day, Superintendent Paramour of the Kent County Constabulary came to the hospital accompanied by Mr J.R. Bingham, a justice of the peace, and at 7 p.m. Paredes made and signed a statement. The very English wording in some parts suggests that this was not taken verbatim, but the information can only have come from the victim, and he made it clear that the attack was racially motivated.

> I, Emilio Paredes, of the American warship 'Sharkey', now lying in the River Thames off Gravesend, Kent, do hereby solemnly and sincerely declare that I believe I am dying, and have no hope of recovery. I went to St Mark's dance last night, the 26th August inst., about 9.15 p.m. When I got into the dance, three American sailors by the name of Smith, Coffer and Anderson were there. I realize while we were dancing they did not like us to be mixed up with the dance, because we are Phillipinos [sic]. The dance closed exactly at 11 o'clock, and while we were on our way to the ship these three fellows passed by me, and when they were ten yards in front of me I just heard Smith fire several times, and all I know I fall down. While I was walking I was with three Phillipinos [sic] off the warship 'Lardner' and when I fell down they ran and disappeared, so fortunately two English civilian people picked me up and put me in a 'bus and took me to the Hospital, and that was the last.
> 
> Question: Are you quite sure it was Smith who fired?
> Answer: I am quite sure.
> Question: Do you know why Smith fired at you?
> Answer: Because he hates Phillipinos [sic] – Smith is a gunner on the 'Lardner'.
> E.W. Paredes.

*Gravesend Hospital. (Author's collection)*

The accused man, Le Bon Emmanuel Smith, was born in Canton, South Carolina on 25 May 1898. His father, Alfred, was a labourer, and Le Bon was the eighth of twelve children. In 1920 when the family was living in Broome, New York, his sixty-one-year-old father was still working as a labourer, his fifty-four-year-old mother, Annabel, washed dishes in a restaurant and Le Bon was a moulder in a foundry. It was a household in which only the youngest were not expected to earn an income. Smith's later position as a gunner on a US naval vessel must have been a considerable source of pride to his family.

Smith and his associates had returned to their ship after the shooting. The obvious next step was to take Smith into custody for questioning, but when men from the Kent Constabulary led by Superintendent Paramour boarded the *Lardner*, the officers in charge, Lt-Com. Deem and Capt. Paterson, told them that all the sailors who had attended the dance were already in custody on board ship, and refused to give them up. Although the crime had been committed on British soil, and the *Lardner* was anchored in British territorial waters, it was pointed out that the ship itself was American territory over which Britain had no jurisdiction. This conflict between the British and American legal systems had the potential to create international friction, and on 28 August the circumstances of the shooting were reported to the Home Secretary, Sir William Joynson-Hicks. Shortly afterwards, an investigation into the incident was carried out by the American Naval Authorities aboard the USS *Sharkey*, and Superintendent Paramour was permitted to attend. It was obvious from the start that the white sailors and the Filipino sailors would have very different accounts of what had taken place.

Russell H. Coffer, born in Virginia in 1898, was an electrician on the *Lardner*. On the night of 26 August he had left the dance in the company of Smith and Anderson, and they met up with two of the English girls they had seen at the dance, Lucy and Ivy. The little group had passed by some Filipinos in the street, and Coffer said that shortly afterwards he had been struck on the back of the head. The next thing he knew he was lying on the ground and one of the girls was holding him. He was sure that it was one of the Filipinos who had assaulted him. He claimed to know nothing about the shooting. He said that he did not own a gun and had never seen Smith with one.

Vernon Lester Anderson, born in Columbia, South Carolina in 1906, was a seaman first class on the *Lardner*. He stated that six or seven Filipinos had come into the dance hall but no words had been spoken that evening between the two parties. He had left the dance at 11 p.m. with Coffer and Smith and after meeting Lucy and Ivy in the street, they passed by a group of Filipinos. No words had been spoken but one of the Filipinos had hit Coffer on the head. A Filipino called Atendido had also tried to hit Coffer when he was on the ground but Anderson had stopped him. Anderson said he had heard two shots and seen a Filipino fall, but had not seen a flash. He and Smith then took Coffer to the hospital to get the head wound dressed, but on arrival they were told that a Filipino sailor was there. Thinking that all the Filipinos were there with their comrade, the men decided not to go in to avoid any possible trouble. They took Coffer back to the ship, where his head was dressed by the doctor. He thought that the weapon used to hit Coffer was a rock or nut tied up in a handkerchief. Anderson said that neither he nor Smith had a gun though he had seen a knife in the hand of one of the Filipinos.

Bonifacio Barben, born in the Pitcairn Islands in 1899, was the officers' cook on the *Lardner*, and he had left the dance with Paredes and three other Filipinos. After walking for five minutes they reached 'a dark place where there were no houses' and Smith 'fired a shot to that boy'. He didn't see anyone hit Coffer. He said he had run away because he 'did not like to be killed.'

Francisco Atendido, born in 1900 in the Pitcairn Islands, was a mess attendant first class on the *Sharkey* and stated that he had seen Smith take a gun from his pocket and shoot Paredes. When the shooting happened Anderson had said, 'Come on! Killed him! Killed him!' He thought there were five shots in all. Atendido denied hitting Coffer. He said he had run about a mile after the shooting and had not gone to help Paredes because he was 'scared'.

Narciso Gavilo, born in 1901 in the Pitcairn Islands, was a mess attendant third class on the *Sharkey*. He had heard five shots, and recognised Smith as the man who had fired the gun.

Smith was present at the investigation, and was represented by an officer, but was not questioned. The revolver had not been found. The question of jurisdiction was still under discussion between the British Foreign Office and Washington when, on 31 August, everything changed. In Gravesend Hospital, Emilio Paredes died. On the same day – and whether this was before or after it was known that Paredes had died is unclear – the American vessels, including the *Lardner* and the *Sharkey*, sailed for Spain, taking with them not only the accused man but all the American and Filipino witnesses to the incident.

As he sailed away from the scene of the crime, Smith's fate was being debated by the Home Office and the US Ambassador, Alanson B. Houghton. Houghton had applied to the Home Office requesting that no English warrant should be executed against Smith, and gave his assurance that the prisoner would be dealt with in accordance with the United States Navy Court-Martial Regulations. After some thought, the Home Secretary agreed to this course of action, 'as a matter of international courtesy.' When a question was asked in parliament he stated that in the 'special circumstances of the case, a United States tribunal would be the more convenient court.' The Home Office issued a statement declaring that the decision had been made bearing in mind that both Smith and Paredes belonged to the United States Navy, and that no British subject was directly concerned.

Despite the lack of witnesses, the inquest was held at Gravesend Town Hall on Thursday 1 September before Mr G. Evans Penman, the borough coroner. The jury foreman was a Mr H. Mott. The court was told that on the evening of 26 August, Paredes, a mess attendant second class, had gone with some other Filipinos to a dance at St Mark's Social Club, Rosherville. It had been alleged that when returning from the dance one of the Filipinos had struck an American sailor with a stone knotted into a handkerchief, and one of three American sailors had turned around and shot Paredes. The coroner made it clear to the jury that if they should find a verdict of murder or manslaughter he would issue a warrant for the arrest of the man who had fired the shot.

The first witness was John Preston Dougton, a US Consul, who confirmed the identity of the dead man, and said that although Paredes was from Tondo in the Philippines and not a US citizen he was entitled to US protection.

Lucy M. Kielty of Robert Street, Gravesend, was a married woman whose husband was serving with the King's Own Yorkshire Light Infantry in India. She had attended the dance at St Mark's Social Club on 26 August together with a friend, Ivy Victoria Cole. They had arrived at eight o' clock and the American and Filipino sailors had arrived later. During the evening she had danced with 'white sailors, coloured sailors and civilians'. She said that none of the Americans had said anything to her that suggested they did not like the Filipinos being present.

'As far as you could see,' said the coroner, 'during the evening there was no ill-feeling evinced between the whites and the blacks?'

'They did not associate,' said Lucy.

'Do you mean the coloured seamen kept in one part of the room and the white men in another?' asked the coroner, pointedly.

'Yes.'

Lucy said the dance finished at about a quarter to eleven and she and Ivy left about ten minutes later by the back exit which took them into Beresford Road. As they walked up towards London Road they saw the three American sailors walk across the junction. When the women reached London Road they saw the Filipinos just around the corner by the garage. They were in a group and Ivy walked through them while Lucy walked around. She heard a scuffle and saw Coffer fall, and his friends went to pick him up. Immediately afterwards she heard two or three shots. According to Lucy, she and Ivy were on the pavement and the Americans were in the road 2 or 3ft in front of them. Despite this, she said she had not seen any of the Americans fire a shot. The coroner cautioned her but she stuck to her story, saying she had seen no spark or flash, and thought the shot had come from somewhere behind her.

'Do you mean to tell me that you do not think the men in the road, either of the white sailors, fired the shot?' asked the coroner, incredulously.

'I do not think so or I think I would have seen them,' replied Lucy. Following the shooting she and Ivy had walked down the road, and turning back saw Coffer staggering along. She asked if he was hurt and he had replied, 'No; only a nasty smack on the back of the head.' His head was bleeding and she gave him her handkerchief. She and Ivy walked down the road with him and the other two Americans came up and asked if he was hurt. She directed them to the nearby hospital.

'I cannot help thinking that you are keeping something back,' said the coroner, but Lucy said, 'no.' After some further questions he remarked, with obvious disgruntlement, 'I must be satisfied with that but it seems an extraordinary thing to me that you were within 3ft of the man alleged to have fired and yet you did not see anything.'

*London Road, Gravesend, 2008. (Author's collection)*

Ivy Victoria Cole of Terrace Street, Gravesend, was an eighteen-year-old shop assistant. She confirmed that the two parties of sailors had kept to separate parts of the dance floor. When leaving the hall she and Lucy had met up with the American sailors at the top of Beresford Road. At that point the Filipino sailors were a few feet in front of them. She had walked through the group of Filipinos and the Americans had left the path to walk around them. Lucy had joined her, and then there was a scuffle. When asked what she meant by this she said, 'All the sailors seemed to get excited and mixed up together.'

Questioned further, she said it was the 'coloured' sailors who were mixed together while the white sailors were in the roadway, but she didn't look behind her to see what was happening. She didn't see Coffer fall, but she did hear the shots, which seemed to come from behind her. She didn't see who fired.

'A most extraordinary thing,' said Penman with increasing frustration. 'You say you were within a foot of the men, one of whom is alleged to have fired a fatal shot, and yet you say you saw nothing. Your friend says the same. I do not believe a word of it.'

'I was not looking the way the shot came,' protested Ivy.

'That does not matter. You were all together. You told exactly the same tale at the enquiry on the ships. You two girls are the only witnesses I have got, and although you were in the middle of it, you say you saw nothing. You didn't want to see who fired, did you?'

'No, I did not,' she replied.

'So it seems,' he retorted. Penman asked if the Filipinos had attacked the Americans and she replied, 'They must have done.' He asked her again, getting the answer, 'Yes.' The coroner issued a stern lecture to Ivy, saying that he was certain that she had not told him the whole truth, and that if she had committed perjury she would be liable to be sent to prison. Ivy stuck determinedly to her story.

Lucy and Ivy might have imagined that since none of the sailors were present at the inquest, there would be no contradiction to their version of events, but they were about to receive an unpleasant surprise. After the evidence of George Jenner and Dr Watt, Superintendent Paramour appeared and read out not only the dying statement of Emilio Paredes but the evidence given at the investigation on board the *Sharkey*. The jury now knew that Paredes and the three Filipinos had identified Smith as the man who fired the gun, whereas all of the Americans and both the English witnesses claimed they had failed to see anyone fire at all.

The coroner summed up, telling the jury that if they believed the Filipinos the verdict should be 'murder' but if they were unable to justify that conclusion they should return an open verdict, stating that the deceased was killed by a gunshot wound but there was insufficient evidence to say by whom it was fired. The coroner was clearly unimpressed by the failure of the US Navy to give up the suspect. 'I should like to tell you,' he said, 'that the Home Office has been in communication with me over this case, and that it is my intention – and that course was agreed to by the Home Office – that if a verdict of murder or manslaughter is returned, to commit the man concerned as if he were at large, and not under arrest.' The jury retired, and after deliberation they returned a verdict of wilful murder against Le Bon Emmanuel Smith. Penman duly issued a warrant for the arrest of Smith and his committal to take his trial at Maidstone Assizes.

The international negotiations eventually resulted in an agreement that Smith would be tried by US court-martial. In view of the necessity of calling the English witnesses the naval vessels returned to anchor off Gravesend and it was in the tiny ward-room of the *Lardner* that Le Bon Emanuel Smith was tried for the murder of Emilio Paredes, the hearing commencing on 29 October 1926. The president of the court was the Commodore of the flotilla, Capt. William W. Galbraith. The prosecution was conducted by Lt Moses B. Byington, and Smith was defended by Lt R.U.A. Failing. All the officers attended in full dress uniform with their swords. A young sailor was present to take shorthand notes. A representative of *Gravesend Reporter* must also have observed the proceedings, and there were no doubts where his sympathies lay. Smith, he revealed, 'is a typical American, of athletic build, with a frank, open face, and fresh complexion.' According to the correspondent, Smith remained cool and confident throughout the proceedings, which were less formal than a British trial. At one point it was requested that an electric fan be stopped and it was the defendant who calmly rose, walked across the room and switched it off.

The first witness was described in the press as 'a little Filipino mess-boy of poor physique' who was unable to say who had fired the gun. Atendido, however, said that Smith had pulled the gun from his trouser pocket and shot Paredes. He had

*Police constable, 1922. (Courtesy of Kent Police Museum)*

heard Anderson say 'Kill him!' to Smith. When Gavilo also said he had seen Smith fire the shot, the defence suggested to the court that his evidence was unreliable and asked that he be impeached.

When the court re-assembled on the following day the officers appeared in their service uniforms. Jenner gave evidence of how he had taken Paredes to hospital. He had also given evidence at the original on-board enquiry, and had something to say on the matter. While waiting on deck he had seen Coffer make a sign to Ivy Cole, placing his finger to his lips as if warning her to be silent. Under questioning he admitted that Ivy had first attempted to speak to Coffer.

When Superintendent Paramour gave evidence that Paredes had identified Smith as his assailant, the defence naturally wished to call into question the accuracy of this statement and asked, 'Was any attempt made to have Smith present when Paredes made his dying declaration?'

'Yes,' said Paramour, solemnly, 'but we were informed that Smith could not leave the ship.'

Mr G. Ennis, of The Terrace, Gravesend, was the caretaker of Christ Church Hall, where social events were held. A few days before the murder, Smith and two of his friends had visited the hall, and complained to Ennis about the presence there of a Filipino sailor. One said, 'In our country we do not permit these people to mix with us.' Ennis pointed out that the Filipino was sober and well-behaved, and that American customs did not apply in the United Kingdom. The white sailors persisted, even volunteering to refund the Filipino's entrance fee if he was told to leave. The Filipino, overhearing the conversation, became agitated, saying that the white sailors were shipmates of his and what they were saying was 'all piffle'. Eventually he left the hall voluntarily, but took Ennis' name and address as a witness in case the matter caused trouble later on.

Once the evidence for the prosecution was in, the court adjourned to the following Monday for the defence to make its case. Russell Coffer repeated what he had said at the enquiry, adding that it was he and Anderson who had accompanied Smith to Christ Church Hall. Coffer had told the Filipino, 'Why don't you stay with your own colour' and the Filipino replied that he would take up the matter with his captain. The next day a ship's officer had told Coffer that he had been trying to censor a dance, and that he could not get away with it as the laws in England were different.

*Lt Moses B. Byington (on left of picture). (Author's collection)*

If he went to a place where there were Filipinos and he didn't like it, then he should just leave. Coffer had passed this on to Smith and Anderson. 'We decided we would not bother any more about Filipinos,' he said. He explained the signal he was said to have made to Ivy, stating it was actually meant for Lucy and indicated only that he would not discuss the case with her. Coffer said Smith had no pistol that night. He had heard the shots but assumed they were meant for himself and his friends.

Lucy smiled at Smith as she walked to the witnesses' chair. Giving her occupation as 'a help' she told the same story as at the inquest. The judge advocate asked her if she knew the meaning of perjury. She said she did. Once again she was asked if she knew who had fired the shot, and still she said she did not know, even though she admitted she had been only 3ft from the white sailors.

Ivy was adamant that she had seen nothing at all. She had not even been curious about the shots, which she had assumed were 'a motor bike's tyre going off', and claimed she did not even know there had been a shooting until she had got to the hospital door with Coffer.

Anderson said that the Filipinos were swinging handkerchiefs with weighted ends, and claimed that the Filipinos did all the fighting and the white sailors kept out of their reach.

Chief Inspector J.A. Chambers of the Gravesend Borough Police said that he had been unable to trace the purchase of a revolver by an American before the tragedy. Asked if there was anything prejudicial known about the characters of Lucy and Ivy he said that there was not.

Verdale O. Robinson was the chief pharmacist's mate of the *Lardner*, and testified that Coffer's head had been injured. He had not enquired as to the cause of the injury 'because he presumed that it was an ordinary shore fight.' He thought that Coffer would have been dazed by the blow.

Le Bon Emanuel Smith was called to give evidence. He said that on the night of the shooting he, Coffer and Anderson had walked along the sidewalk just behind the two girls. They caught up with the group of Filipinos who were walking more slowly and occupied most of the sidewalk. He, Coffer, Anderson and one of the girls stepped out into the roadway to pass them by, and just as they stepped back on the sidewalk, Coffer was struck and fell. Smith went to help him but Coffer stood up, and then Smith turned to face the Filipinos. As he did so he heard two shots, and the Filipinos ran away. Later he accompanied Coffer to the hospital. Cross-examined he said he did not see where the shots came from, and thought they must have been 30-50ft away. He stated that the shooting was not discussed on the way to the hospital, or on the way back to the ship. 'No sir, it was not mentioned until the officer woke us up aboard ship.' Smith denied that he, Coffer or Anderson had guns with them. Asked if he had ever owned a gun he said he had owned many but not since he had been in the Navy. He had not known that anyone had been shot until he reached the hospital.

In his final address, Byington made the point that after the shots were fired the Filipinos had run away, whereas the white sailors had calmly walked away. Clearly only the white sailors had known that there would be no more shots. It was also remarkable that the white sailors and the girls all said that on the long walk to the hospital the shooting was not discussed. He believed that Smith and Anderson knew a good deal more than was in their testimony. Was it likely that Paredes, knowing he was dying, would implicate an innocent man? If there was collusion between the Filipinos would it not have been Coffer they accused, the man who had had tried to get a Filipino ejected from a dance hall only a few days previously?

Lt Failing, on behalf of Smith, could only suggest that there had been collusion between the Filipinos who hated the white men. It was a weak defence which might well have encouraged the conclusion that a similar point could have been made about the evidence given by the white sailors.

Following the closing addresses the court sat in private for two hours and when it reopened it was announced only that no decision could be given publicly. Smith was not recalled. The *Reporter*'s representative commented that in American Naval Courts, if the accused was found not guilty, then he was brought into the court and told this. The failure to do so indicated that Smith had been found guilty.

On 4 November the court reconvened to deal with disciplinary charges arising out of the tragedy. There was no official announcement, but it was believed that Anderson, as the leading seaman of the group, was to be arraigned for failing to report the occurrence.

The decisions in the case were not published. An exhaustive search of US Naval records has not brought to light a record of the hearings or their outcome, however further light is thrown on the case by a passenger record maintained by the United States immigration service. On 30 December 1926 the SS *President Van Buren* sailed from Marseilles, arriving at Boston on 11 January 1927. The officer in charge was Lt Failing. Amongst the men on board were Vernon Anderson, Francisco Atendido, Narciso Gavilo, and Le Bon Emanuel Smith, all of whom were transferred to Charlestown Prison.

Both the *Sharkey* and the *Lardner* were sold for scrap in 1931. By 1941 Francisco Atendido had returned to the navy, where he worked as a steward. He died in 1964. Le Bon Smith died in New York in December 1951, aged fifty-three. Russell Coffer died in Virginia in February 1970, aged seventy-one. Bonifacio Barben remained in the US Navy, and became a naturalised citizen of the US in 1938. He died in Hennepin in 1984 and is buried at Arlington cemetery. Narciso Gavilo died in Florida on 19 April 1977, aged seventy-four, and Vernon Anderson died in 1995, aged eighty-nine.

# BIBLIOGRAPHY & REFERENCES

## BOOKS

Anon, *All About Ramsgate and Broadstairs* (London; W. Kent & Co., 1864)

Anon, *An account of the examination of Philip Nicholson, before the Lord Mayor; and of the proceedings of the coroner's inquest, relative to the murder of Mr. and Mrs. Bonar, at Chislehurst, Kent, on Monday morning, 31st May, 1813, together with the particulars of the attempt at suicide, made by P. Nicholson* (London; J. Evans & Son, c.1814)

Anon, *An account of the life, trial, confession, and dying words of Philip Nicholson, who was executed on Monday the 23rd of August, 1813, at Penenden Heath, for the murder of Mr. and Mrs. Bonar, at Chislehurst, Kent* (London; T. Batchelor, c.1813)

Anon, *Dreadful murders: The particulars of the horrid murders of Mr. & Mrs. Bonar Camden Place, Chislehurst, in Kent. Giving an account of the cruel manner of the murders ... The conduct of Phillip Nicholson, the servant ... To which is added a mournful copy of verses* (London; J. Pitts, 1814)

Anon, *Reprieve & sentence of the Penge convicts : (paadon [sic] of Alice Rhodes, the 3 Stauntons imprisonment for life): who were sentenced to be hung at Maidstone, on Tuesday Oct. 16th, 1877, for the cruel shocking murder of Harriet Staunton* (Maidstone?, 1877)

Anon, *The Alleged murder at Penge: Committal of four prisoners for wilful murder* (Maidstone?, 1877)

Anon, *The full particulars of the trial, execution, and dying words, of Philip Nicholson, who was executed at Maidstone, on the twenty third of August, 1813, for the murder of Mr. & Mrs. Bonar ... To which is added the trial & execution of Charles Masureaux, etc* (London; Jennings, c.1813)

Anon, *The Life and Trial of the Four Prisoners [i.e. Louis Adolphus Edmund Staunton, Patrick Llewellyn Staunton, Elizabeth Ann Staunton and Alice Rhodes] connected with the Penge Murder [i.e. the murder of Harriet Staunton]* ('Police News' edition, London, G. Purkess, 1877)

Anon, *Thomas Mears and Others: The Canterbury Rioters, 31st May 1838*

Annand, William, Dean of Edinburgh, *A Funeral Elegie, upon the death of George Sonds Esq; &c. Who was killed by his brother, Mr. Freeman Sonds, August the 7th ... 1655 ... Whereunto is annexed a prayer, compiled by his sorrowfull father Sir George Sonds, and used in his family during the life of the said Freeman* (London; John Crowch, 1655)

Atlay, J.B. (ed), *Trial of the Stauntons* [A report of the trial of L. A. E. Staunton, Patrick Llewellyn Staunton, Elizabeth Ann Staunton and Alice Rhodes for the murder of Harriet Staunton] (Edinburgh & London; W. Hodge & Co., 1911)

Boreman, Robert, *A Mirrour of Mercy and Judgement; or, an Exact true narrative of the life and death of Freeman Sonds ... who ... for murthering his elder brother ... was arraigned and condemned at Maidstone, executed there ... 1655* (London, 1655)

Burton, E.G. *The handbook and companion to Ramsgate Margate Broadstairs Kingsgate, Minster etc etc* (Ramsgate; G. Griggs, 1859)

Canterburiensis, *The Life and Extraordinary Times of Sir William Courtenay, Knight of Malta, alias John Nichols Tom* (Canterbury; James Hunt, 1838)

Clarke, Sir Edward KC 'Leaves from a Lawyer's Case-book. The Penge Mystery', *The Cornhill Magazine* vol. XXXVIII new series, January to June pp. 459-476 (1915)

Clarke, Sir Edward KC 'Leaves from a Lawyer's Case-book. The Case of Esther Pay', *The Cornhill Magazine* vol. XXXVIII new series, January to June pp. 58-69 (1915)

Clarke, Sir Edward KC, *The Story of My Life* (London; John Murray, 1918)

Faber, Richard, *A Brother's Murder* (Faversham; The Faversham Society, c. 1993)

Hastings, Macdonald *The Other Mr Churchill* (London; Four Square, 1966)

Hawkins, Sir Henry, and Harris, Richard, KC (ed.) *The Reminiscences of Sir Henry Hawkins* (London; Thomas Nelson & Sons, 1904)

Hay, Tempest, *Lees Court, an Investigation into its History and Architecture* (Faversham; The Faversham Society, 1997)

Jackson, Stanley *Mr Justice Avory* (London; Victor Gollancz Ltd, 1935)

Marjoribanks, Edward *The Life of Sir Edward Marshall Hall, KC* (London; Victor Gollancz Ltd, 1930)

Meyerstein, Edward Harry William, *A New Ballad of Anne Delaune and Freeman Sondes her lover 1655* (Metcalfe & Cooper; London, 1923)

O'Donnell, Bernard *The Trials of Mr Justice Avory* (London; Rich & Cowan, 1935)

Rogers, P.G., *Battle in Bossenden Wood* (London; Readers Union, Oxford University Press, 1961)

Sondes, Freeman, *The Devils Reign upon Earth: being a relation of several sad and bloudy murthers lately committed, especially that of Sir Geo. Sonds his son [i.e. Freeman Sondes] upon his own brother, etc* (London, 1655)

Sondes, George, Earl of Feversham, *Authentic Memorials of remarkable occurrences and affecting calamities in the family of Sir George Sondes. In two parts. The first being his own narrative; The second the narrative of persons attendant upon his son Freeman Sondes Esq. [during his imprisonment and at his execution* [Compiled by R. Boreman] (Evesham; J. Agg, c. 1790)

Sondes, George, Earl of Feversham, *Sir George Sondes; his plaine narrative to the world of all passages upon the death of his two Sonnes* (London, 1655)

# NEWSPAPERS

*Canterbury Journal and Farmer's Gazette*
*Chatham News and North Kent Spectator*
*Daily Mail*
*Daily Telegraph*
*Everybody's Weekly*
*Faversham Mercury*
*Faversham News and East Kent Journal*
*Good Housekeeping*
*Gravesend Reporter*
*Kentish Gazette*
*Kentish Gazette and Canterbury Times*
*Kent Herald*
*Kentish Observer*
*Maidstone and Kentish Journal*
*Maidstone Gazette and Kentish Chronicle*
*Medical Examiner*
*New York Times*
*Penny Illustrated Paper*
*Saturday Review*
*Sydenham Forest Hill and Penge Gazette*
*The Illustrated Police News*
*The People*
*The Times*
*Windsor and Eton Express*
*Whitstable Times and Tankerton Press*

# RECORDS

PRO/KEW: HO 144/26/64091C
PRO/KEW: TS 18/3
PRO/KEW: J 77/291/8617
PRO/KEW: CRIM 1/35/3
*The Newgate Calendar*, ex-classics edition
Probate records

# WEBSITES

www.ancestry.com
www.exclassics.com

# INDEX

Aldridge, Mr 59
Amos, George Adam 114, 115, 116, 124
Anderson, Vernon Lester 145, 146, 147, 148, 149, 150, 151, 152, 153, 154
Andrews, Mr 71, 75-6
Angerstein, John, jnr 25, 26, 28
Angerstein, John, snr 25, 26
Armstrong, Major 47
Atendido, Francisco 146, 147, 148, 149, 150, 153, 154
Avory, Mr Justice 135, 138, 139, 140, 141

Baker, Stephen 48
Barben, Bonifacio 147, 148, 149, 150, 153, 154
Barrow, Mr 74, 75, 76
Barton, Charles 104
Barton, James Browning 133, 137, 139, 140
Barwood, Frederick 130
Bateman, Sergeant Joseph 89
Bawden, Stephen 105
Bennett, Lt 47, 48, 49
Bingham, J.R. 145
Biron, Robert 106, 112
Bonar, Anne (*née* Thomson) 21, 22, 23, 24, 25, 26, 28, 29, 30
Bonar, Henry 25, 32
Bonar, Thomson jnr 25, 29, 30, 31, 32, 33
Bonar, Thomson snr 21, 22, 23, 24, 25, 26, 28, 29, 30, 32
Bond, Dr 100
Boreman, Robert 16
Bossenden Farm 42, 43, 45, 47, 48
Bossenden Wood 46, 47
Boswell, Dr J. Irvine 118, 121, 122
Bowes, Dr Charles 118
Bramston, Mr 29, 32, 33
Branchett, George 48
Brasier, John 57, 59-60
Bright, John Edward 89
Brown, Clara 82, 83, 84, 85, 89, 90, 91, 93, 94, 95
Bugden, John 57
Bullard, Robert 105
Burford, Mrs 49
Burford, William 47, 48, 49
Burton, Ann 75, 76, 78-9
Burton, Robert Alexander 68, 69, 71, 72, 73, 74, 75, 76, 77, 78, 79, 80
Burton, Thomas 71, 78
Butterfield, Harriet (*née* Suter) 81, 82, 85, 86, 87, 88, 89, 93, 94
Butterfield, Revd 86
Byington, Lt Moses B. 150, 154

Callahan, Eugene 52, 55
Camden Place, Chislehurst 21, 25, 27
Camden, Lord 28
Campbell, Mr Scarlet 95
Carroll, Miss 109
Carttar, Mr 89, 90

Casabianca, Ellen, (*née* Richardson) 81, 88
Casabianca, Louis Victor 88
Castlereagh, Lord 28-9
Catt, George 46, 47, 48, 49
Chalklin, Mrs 87
Challis, George 56, 57
Chambers, Chief Inspector J.A. 153
Chatham Lines 66, 67, 69, 73
Churchill, Robert 139, 141, 142
Clarke, Eliza 97, 99, 100, 103, 104, 110, 111
Clarke, Mary 22, 23, 24
Clarke, Sir Edward 81, 92, 93, 96, 106, 108, 109, 110, 111
Clarke, Walter 97, 99, 111
Clarke, William 71, 72, 73
Coffer, Russell H. 145, 146, 147, 148, 149, 150, 151, 152, 153, 154
Cohen, Arthur Sefton 134
Cole, Ivy Victoria 146, 148, 149, 150, 151, 153
Coltrupp, Thomas 39
Cooper, Astley 24, 25, 26, 28, 29
Cope, Revd Richard 40
Courtenay, Sir William Percy Honywood 36, 37, 38, 39, 40, 41, 42, 43, 44, 45, 46, 47, 48, 49
Creasey, Dr 86, 87, 92
Crisp, Edmund 12, 15
Cronk, Charles 104
Crook, Judge 14
Culver, Sarah 42, 43, 45, 48
Curling, Edward 48
Curling, Henry 54, 57, 61, 63
Curling, Mr 43, 46
Curnick, Susannah 22, 23
Cussens, Sergeant 101, 102

Dale, Mr 25, 26, 31
Daniell, John Mortlock 64
Day, Alice 109, 110
Deacon, George 71
Deem, Lt Commander 146
Delaune, Anne 8, 9
Denton, Emma 82, 90
Derham, Consuelo (*née* de Colegan) 128
Derham, John Adam Tytler 128, 129, 130, 131, 132, 133, 134, 136, 138, 139, 140, 141
Derham, Matilda 129, 130, 134
Derham, Walter 128, 134
Devon, Earl of 36, 41
Dewberry, George 84
Dickens, Henry Fielding 126, 127
Dougton, John Preston 148
Dunkin, John 43
Dunn, Richard 114
Duras, Lady Mary (*née* Sondes) 20
Duras, Lord 20
Dutton, Thomas Duerdin 103, 104, 106

East Cliff Lodge 52
Edwards, Daniel 43, 44, 46

# INDEX

Emmerson, R.J. 55
Ennis, G. 152
Everist, Superintendent 68, 69, 71, 73
Everist, Thomas 67
Evers, Dr 121, 122

Faber, Richard 7
Failing, Lt R.U.A. 150, 151, 154
Fairbrook Farm 39, 42, 46
Fayle, Dr Higginson 76, 77-8
Fisher, Sergeant 67
Flower, Alderman Sir Charles 26
Foad, Alexander 48, 49
Folds, Penelope 23
Forrester, Officer 26, 27
Foster, Mr 12, 14
Foster, William 48
Fowle, Inspector 116, 117, 118, 119-120, 121, 125, 126
Francis, George 39, 41, 42, 43, 46
Freeman, Sir Ralph 5

Galbraith, Captain William W. 150
Gant, Frederick 63-4
Gavilo, Narciso 147, 148, 149, 150, 151, 153, 154
Gibbs, Matilda 57
Gibbs, Samuel 57, 60, 62, 63
Gibson, F.G. 114, 116
Gilbert, Mr 67
Gooding, Nurse Ellen 87
Green, Thomas 58-9
Grey, Sir George 78
Griggs, George 48
Groves, Colonel 43
Gye, Mr 90, 93

Hadlow, Henry 45
Hadlow, Mrs 43, 45
Hales Place 36
Hales, Baronet 36
Hall, Sir Edward Marshall, KC 137, 138, 139, 140, 141
Handley, Major 46
Handley, Revd 41, 46
Hardy, Charles 134
Harman, Mr 89
Harold, Mr 76
Harrington, Arthur 97, 103, 110
Harris, E.C. 134
Harris, Emma 99, 100, 103, 104, 110-111
Harris, W.J. 122, 125
Harrower, David 131, 138
Harvey, Phineas 48
Hawkins, Sir Henry 91, 93, 94, 127
Heath, Mr Justice 30, 32
Hibbert, Constable Stephen 68
Hill, Constable James 97-9, 103
Hill, Dr William Reed 118
Hills, T. 68
Holland, Constable Alfred 86
Holt, Mr 28
Holy Cross Church, Bearsted 16, 34
Honywood, Sir John Courtenay 36
Houghton, Alanson B. 147
Houghton, George 66, 67
Houghton, Lucy 66, 68, 72, 73, 79
Houghton, Thomas Frederick 66, 67, 68-9, 72, 79
Houghton, William 66, 79
Humphrey, James 100, 101
Humphrey, Mary 106, 110, 111
Humphrey, William 106, 111

Ilott, Thomas 24
Irwin, Mrs 109, 110

Jackson, George 60
Jenner, George Edwin 143, 150, 151
Johns, John 59, 63
Jordan, William 59
Joynson-Hicks, Sir William 146, 147
Judd, Thomas 105, 111

Keene, Thomas 83, 85
Kemp, Mrs 106, 110, 111
Kent County Lunatic Asylum 40, 43
Kielty, Lucy M. 146, 148, 149, 150, 153
Kimber, Mr 134
King, Charles 22, 29
Kingsford, Stephen 56
Knatchbull, Norton 46, 47
Kydd, Samuel 58, 63

Labatt, Maurice 60
Lang, Mr 110
Large, Mr 100-101
Lavender, Officer 25
Lees Court Sheldwich 5, 6, 7, 9, 10, 20
Livesey, Sir Michael 12
Livick, Supt James 60, 64
Locke, George William 67, 68
Longrigg, Dr Dean 87, 88, 89, 90, 92
Lucas, Mary Jane 57
Lyddon, Charles 113, 114, 115, 116, 117, 118, 119, 120, 121, 122, 123, 124, 125, 126, 127
Lyddon, Dr William Reeks 113, 114, 115, 116, 117, 118, 119, 120, 121, 122, 123, 124, 125, 126, 127
Lyddon, Eliza 113
Lyddon, Elizabeth (previously Twort) 113, 114, 116, 117, 118, 119, 120, 121, 122, 123, 125, 126, 127
Lyddon, John 113, 114
Lyddon, Sarah, (*née* Twort) 113, 115
Lyons, Harry 116
Lyster, Mr 89

Maidment, Mrs 108, 110
Maidstone Gaol 12, 32, 40, 49, 91, 94, 95
Marchant, William 84
Marshall, Inspector 99, 101, 102, 103, 110
Martyr, Mr 27
Mattern, Frederick 52, 54, 55, 56, 57, 58, 59, 60, 61, 62, 63, 64, 65
Mattern, Henry 60, 65
Maxted, Charlotte 60
Mayne, Superintendent 126
Mears, John 43, 44, 46
Mears, Nicholas 43, 44, 45, 46, 48, 49
Mears, Thomas 44, 46, 48, 49
Medhurst, James 56
Mercer, Mr 126
Milgate, Thomas 47
Montefiore, Sir Moses 52, 57
Moore, Georgina 97, 98, 99, 100, 101, 102, 103, 104, 105, 106, 107, 108, 109, 110, 111
Moore, Harry 97, 109, 112
Moore, Mary Elizabeth 97, 98, 100, 101, 102, 104, 109, 110, 112
Moore, Stephen 97, 99, 100, 101, 102, 103, 104, 106, 108, 109, 110, 111, 112
Mott, H. 147
Mowll, A.K. 134
Murphy, Mr, QC 126

# INDEX

Naylor, Charles 116-117, 118, 119, 120, 121, 122, 123, 125, 127
Nettlestead 100, 106
Nicholson, Bridget 28, 30
Nicholson, Patrick 28, 30
Nicholson, Phillip 22, 23, 24, 25, 26, 27, 28, 29, 30, 31, 32, 33, 34
Nines, Charlotte 57, 59-60, 63
Nutting, William 49

Oliver, Roland, KC 136, 138, 139

Paddock Wood 104, 105, 106, 107, 110
Paramour, Superintendent 145, 146, 151
Paredes, Emilio 143, 145, 146, 147, 148, 149, 150, 151, 153, 154
Partridge, Mr 103
Paterson, Captain 146
Pay, Esther 97, 98, 99, 100, 101, 102, 103, 104, 105, 106, 107, 108, 109, 110, 111, 112
Pay, William 97, 99, 100, 101, 102, 108, 109, 111, 112
Payne, Alfred 43
Penenden Heath 16, 33, 34
Penhorn, Alfred 100
Penman, G. Evans 147, 148, 148, 149, 150
Piggott, Mr 89
Poland, Sir Harry Bodkin 103, 104, 106, 107, 111, 112
Pollock, Mr Baron 106, 111
Poore, Dr 43, 46, 47
Poynder, Mr 41, 43
Price, William 42, 44, 46, 49
Prichard, Superintendent 60
Prout, Hannah 105

Quested, Sergeant 134, 135, 139

Randall, Mr 23
Reeves, Mr 27
Reid, Captain 47
Rhodes, Alice 82, 84, 85, 86, 87, 90, 91, 93, 94, 95, 96
Rhodes, Lewis Staunton 91
Ribton, William 73, 74, 75, 76
Riddell, William 59, 60, 62
Rivers, Inspector 134, 139
Rivers, Lady 81
Rivers, Lord 81, 88
Roberts, Mr 28
Robinson, Verdale O. 153
Rockingham, Countess Katherine (née Sondes) 20
Rockingham, Earl of 20
Rogers, Professor 92
Royal Oak Hotel, Ramsgate 56, 58
Russell, Dr 90
Russell, Lord John 41, 49, 51
Rutter, Caroline 97, 99, 100, 103-4, 110, 111
Rutter, James 99, 103
Rye, William 48

Sandwell, William Danton 59
Sargent, Sergeant Frederick 121, 125
Seymour, Lord Robert 28
Smith, Alfonso Francis Austin 128, 129, 130, 131, 132, 133, 134, 135, 136, 137, 138, 139, 140, 141, 142
Smith, Alfred 146
Smith, Annabel 146
Smith, Jackie 131, 142
Smith, Le Bon Emmanuel 143, 145, 146, 147, 148, 149, 150, 151, 152, 153, 154
Smith, Mr, of Chislehurst 25
Smith, Rosina Ivy (née Wight) aka Kathleen 128, 129, 130, 131, 132, 133, 134, 135, 138, 139, 140, 141, 142
Smith, Ruth Bernadette, (née Wynne) 128, 142
Smith, Sir Frank 128
Solley, Mr 61
Sondes, Freeman I 5
Sondes, Freeman II 5, 7-16
Sondes, George 5, 7-15
Sondes, Jane (née Freeman) 5, 6, 7
Sondes, Mary (née Villiers) 20
Sondes, Nicholas 9-10
Sondes, Sir George 5-16, 20
Spratt, John 48
St Augustine's Gaol, Canterbury 48, 126
St Michael and All Angels, Throwley 12
Staples, John 85
Staunton, Elizabeth Ann (née Rhodes) 82, 83, 85-96
Staunton, Harriet (née Richardson) 81, 82, 83, 84, 85, 86, 87, 88, 89, 90, 91, 92, 93, 95
Staunton, Louis 81, 82, 83, 84, 85, 86, 87, 88, 89, 90, 91, 92, 93, 94, 95, 96
Staunton, Patrick Llewellyn snr 82, 83, 85, 86, 87, 88, 89, 90, 91, 92, 93, 94, 95, 96
Staunton, Patrick Llewellyn jnr 91
Staunton, Thomas Henry 82, 83, 85, 86, 90-1, 92, 93, 94
*Stella Maris* 130, 131, 132, 133, 141
Stephen, Sir James 91
Stevenson, Thomas 122
Stiles, Sir Thomas 12
Straight, Douglas 93
Stroud, Thomas 36, 39
Stroud, W. 55
Suter, Eleanor 81

Tom, Charity 40
Tom, John Nichols (see Courtenay, Sir William Percy Honywood)
Tom, Mrs Catharine (née Fulpitt) 40
Tom, William 40
Tree, Albert 67
Tyrrell, Frederick 32

Uridge, Elizabeth 86, 89

Vivian, Sir Hussey 41, 49

Waghorn, George 105
Watt, Dr 143, 150
Webster, Mr 54
Wells, George 86
Wells, Mr 29
Westgate Gaol, Canterbury 39
Whitney, Dr 133-4, 138, 139
Wiggins, John J. 118, 119, 120, 122, 123, 126
Wight, Lillian 130, 131, 132, 133, 134
Wightman, Mr Justice 74-5, 76-7, 78
Wilkinson, F.E. 89
Wilkinson, Thomas 52
Williams, Montagu 93
Wills, William 42, 43, 48, 49
Wise, Sarah 125
Wood, Dr 100
Woodruff, Mr 121
Woolmer, Charles Edward Shirley 77, 79
Wraight, Edward sen 48
Wraight, Edward, jun 48
Wyatt, Miss 130
Wynne, Robert John 128

Yalding 100, 101, 104, 106, 107, 109, 110, 111